Additional Practice Workbook

GRADE 4 TOPICS 1–16

enVision® Mathematics

SAVVAS
LEARNING COMPANY

ISBN-13: 978-0-134-95379-3
ISBN-10:   0-134-95379-7
9   22

Grade 4 Topics 1–16

Name _____

Additional Practice 1-1
Numbers Through One Million

Another Look!

A place-value chart can help you read greater numbers. This chart has three periods: millions, thousands, and ones.

According to a recent census, the city of Boston was home to 625,087 people. Each digit of 625,087 is written in its place on the chart.

You can write the number in expanded form and using its number name.

600,000 + 20,000 + 5,000 + 80 + 7

six hundred twenty-five thousand, eighty-seven

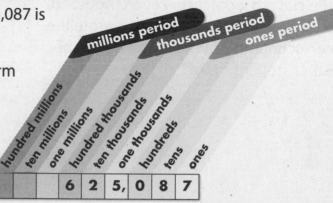

1. Write six hundred twelve thousand, three hundred in the place-value chart. Then write the number in expanded form.

2. Write forty-one thousand, two hundred eleven in the place-value chart. Then write the number in expanded form.

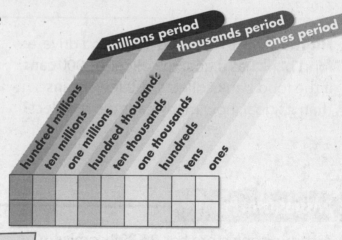

For **3–5**, write each number in expanded form.

3. 500,000

4. 64,672

5. 99,327

For **6–8**, write the number names.

6. 92,318

7. 428,737

8. 8,216

9. Jackson has 5 boxes of 3 golf balls. Elsa gives Jackson 2 more boxes of 3 golf balls. How many golf balls does Jackson have now?

10. Thirty-five thousand, four hundred seventeen people attended a county fair. Write this number using numerals.

11. Construct Arguments The teacher asks the class to write forty-seven thousand, twenty-seven. Which student wrote the correct number? What mistake did the other student make?

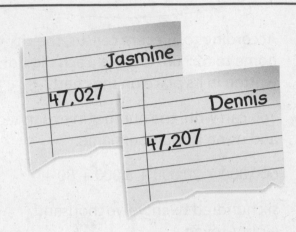

Jasmine
47,027

Dennis
47,207

12. Higher Order Thinking At a food drive, a food bank has a goal to collect 24,000 cans. If the food bank collects 100 fewer cans than its goal, how many cans did it collect?

Think about which place values have to change.

Assessment Practice

13. A comic book store has 26,298 comics in stock. Select all the places in 26,298 that have the digit 2.

- ☐ ones
- ☐ tens
- ☐ hundreds
- ☐ thousands
- ☐ ten thousands

14. Select all that are equal to 209,604.

- ☐ 200,000 + 9,000 + 604
- ☐ 200,000 + 9,000 + 600 + 4
- ☐ 29,000 + 600 + 4
- ☐ 200,000 + 9,000 + 60 + 4
- ☐ 209,000 + 600 + 4

Name _____

Another Look!

Aria earned 13 scout badges in one year. Her whole troop earned ten times that number of badges. How many badges did Aria's troop earn?

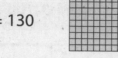

13 × 10 = 130

13 badges

130 badges

100 is ten times as great as 10, and 30 is ten times as great as 3.

Aria's troop earned 130 badges all together.

1. Write the value of the digit in the hundreds place and the value of the digit in the tens place in 440. What is the relationship between the values of those two digits?

440

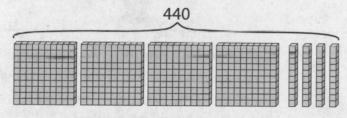

The _____ in the hundreds place has a value _____ times as great as the _____ in the _____ place.

_____   _____

2. Write a number in which the value of the 8 is ten times greater than the value of the 8 in 8,304.

For **3–4**, use the relationship between the values of the digits to solve.

3. On the first day of the clothing drive, 11 rain jackets were collected. At the end of the drive, 10 times that number of rain jackets were collected. How many rain jackets were collected?

4. After the clothing drive had ended, volunteers placed the 2,000 items collected into 10 piles to go to ten different shelters. How many items were in each pile?

5. What is the relationship between the 6s in 675,002 and 385,621?

6. Name the value of each 2 in 222,222.

For **7–8**, use the graph at the right.

7. Who sold the most cups of lemonade? Who sold the fewest?

8. Algebra How many cups of lemonade were sold in all? Write and solve an equation.

---

9. Reasoning Is the relationship between the 7s in 7,742 and the 7s in 7,785 different in any way? Explain.

10. Higher Order Thinking In your own words, explain the place-value relationship when the same two digits are next to each other in a multi-digit number.

Assessment Practice

11. Which of the following shows the values of the 5s in 15,573?

(A) 500 and 5

(B) 500 and 50

(C) 5,000 and 50

(D) 5,000 and 500

12. In which number is the value of the 6 ten times as great as the value of the 6 in 162,398?

(A) 465,871

(B) 596,287

(C) 645,010

(D) 754,699

Name _____

Additional Practice 1-3
Compare Whole Numbers

Another Look!

Which distance is greater: the moon's distance from Earth on February 7 or its distance from Earth on March 5?

Which place value can you use to compare the numbers?

March 5
227,011 miles

February 7
229,909 miles

Write the numbers, lining up the places. Begin at the left and compare.	Continue comparing the digits from left to right.	The first place where the digits are different is the thousands place.
229,909 227,011	229,909 227,011	229,909 227,011
The hundred thousands digit is the same in both numbers.	The ten thousands digit is the same in both numbers.	Compare. 9 thousands > 7 thousands, so 229,909 > 227,011 The moon's distance from Earth is greater on February 7.

For **1–8**, complete by writing >, =, or < in each ◯.

1. 854,376 ◯ 845,763

2. 52,789 ◯ 52,876

3. 944,321 ◯ 940,123

4. 59,536 ◯ 59,536

5. 3,125 ◯ 4,125

6. 418,218 ◯ 41,821

7. 70,000 + 2,000 ◯ 70,000 + 200

8. 34,000 + 74 ◯ 30,000 + 4,000 + 70 + 4

For **9–14**, write which place to use when comparing the numbers.

9. 3,176
   3,472

10. 899,451
    756,451

11. 28,119
    28,124

12. 94,283
    96,281

13. 1,983
    1,982

14. 490,165
    390,264

15. Use < or > to write a comparison between 2 of the city populations shown in the table.

City Populations	
Hauserberg	129,616
Devinsville	128,741
Mandel Village	129,788

16. (A-Z) **Vocabulary** A number written in expanded form is written as the sum of each _____. Write 39,005 in expanded form.

17. **Reasoning** According to the 2010 census, the state with the fewest people is Wyoming, with a population of 563,626. Write the number that is ten thousand greater than 563,626.

18. **Higher Order Thinking** Celia writes the addition problems shown. She says she can tell which sum will be greater without adding. How does Celia know?

$8,157 + 364$

$8,157 + 519$

19. Find the sums. Write a comparison using >, <, or =.

Assessment Practice

20. Is each comparison true or false?

	True	False
356,019 < 357,000	☐	☐
219,475 > 219,476	☐	☐
54,233 > 44,233	☐	☐

21. Is each comparison true or false?

	True	False
909,909 > 990,909	☐	☐
41,032 > 41,023	☐	☐
19,231 < 19,312	☐	☐

6   **Topic 1** | Lesson 1-3

Name _____

Another Look!

The population for Jacksonville, FL in 2010 was 821,784. Round the population to the nearest ten, hundred, thousand, ten thousand, and hundred thousand.

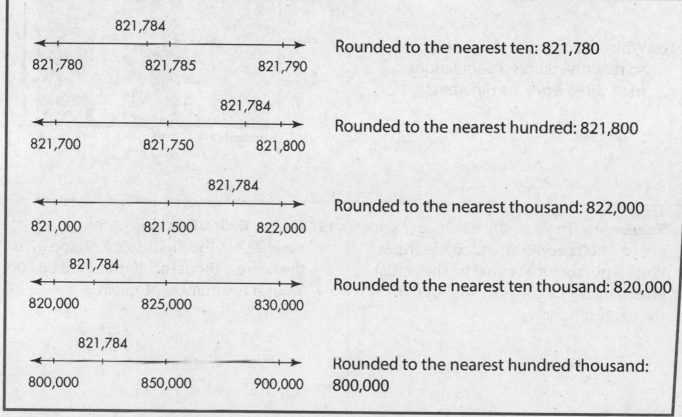

821,784

| 821,780 | 821,785 | 821,790 |

Rounded to the nearest ten: 821,780

821,784

| 821,700 | 821,750 | 821,800 |

Rounded to the nearest hundred: 821,800

821,784

| 821,000 | 821,500 | 822,000 |

Rounded to the nearest thousand: 822,000

821,784

| 820,000 | 825,000 | 830,000 |

Rounded to the nearest ten thousand: 820,000

821,784

| 800,000 | 850,000 | 900,000 |

Rounded to the nearest hundred thousand: 800,000

For **1–16**, use place value or a number line to round each number to the place of the underlined digit.

1. 1̲60,656

2. 1̲49,590

3. 117,8̲21

4. 7̲5,254

5. 2,4̲20

6. 900,98̲5

7. 4̲40,591

8. 2̲05,000

9. 58̲,365

10. 1,8̲76

11. 61,2̲29

12. 7̲,849

13. 8̲67,867

14. 10̲,811

15. 49,9̲51

16. 251,38̲2

17. **enVision® STEM** Use the data in the graph at the right.

a. Which place could you round to so that the rounded populations of all three cities are the same?

b. Which place could you round to so that the rounded populations of all three cities are different?

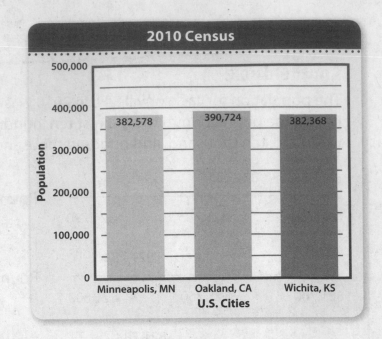

2010 Census

Minneapolis, MN 382,578
Oakland, CA 390,724
Wichita, KS 382,368

U.S. Cities

18. **Reasoning** The box office manager said about 5,000 people attended the show. Write a number that could be the actual attendance if he correctly rounded to the nearest hundred.

19. **Higher Order Thinking** A 5-digit number has the digits 0, 5, 7, 9, and 0. To the nearest thousand, it rounds to 80,000. What is the number? Explain.

☑ **Assessment Practice**

20. Complete the table. Round each number to the given place.

Number	Hundred	Thousand	Ten Thousand	Hundred Thousand
155,999				
399,411				
817,031				
114,712				
909,843				

Another Look!

In a recent year, Colorado issued 23,301 building permits and Vermont issued 2,296 building permits. Kyle said Colorado issued about 100 times as many permits as Vermont.

Tell how you can construct an argument to justify whether or not Kyle's conjecture is true.

- I can decide if the conjecture makes sense.

- I can use numbers to explain my reasoning.

Construct an argument to justify whether or not Kyle's conjecture is true.

Kyle's conjecture is not true. Rounding to the nearest ten thousand, Colorado issued about 20,000 building permits. Vermont issued about 2,000 permits, rounding to the nearest thousand. One hundred times 2,000 is 200,000, so Colorado issued only about ten times as many building permits as Vermont, not 100 times as many.

When you construct arguments, you use numbers and symbols correctly to explain.

Construct Arguments

Alisa says it is easier to compare the numbers in Set A than the numbers in Set B.

1. What is one way you could construct an argument justifying whether Alisa's conjecture is true?

DATA	Set A	Set B
	45,760	492,111
	1,025,680	409,867

2. Is Alisa's conjecture true? Justify your answer.

3. Alisa wrote a comparison for Set B using the ten thousands place. Explain what strategy she could have used.

Flight Distances

Chicago O'Hare is a busy international airport. The map shows the flight distance from Chicago O'Hare to several cities. Lee conjectured the flight distance from Chicago to Istanbul is the same as the flight distance from Chicago to Sao Paulo when the distances are rounded to the nearest thousand.

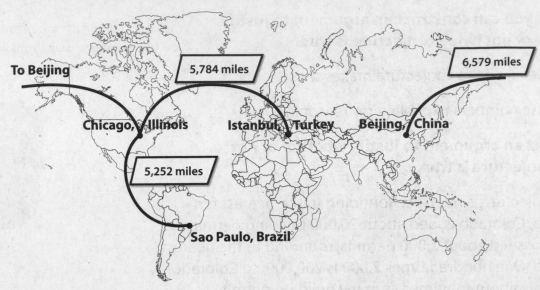

4. **Construct Arguments** Describe at least one way you could construct an argument justifying Lee's conjecture.

When you construct arguments, you can use place-value understanding.

5. **Be Precise** How can you round the two flight distances in Lee's conjecture?

6. **Reasoning** Is Lee's conjecture true? Justify your answer.

Name _____

Another Look!

Mental math strategies work because of the properties of operations.

Addition Strategies

Find 3,928 + 2,480 with mental math.

Make Ten

Use the Associative Property of Addition.
$$3,928 + 2,480 = (3,408 + 520) + 2,480$$
$$= 3,408 + (520 + 2,480)$$
$$= 3,408 + 3,000 = 6,408$$

Add On

Use the Communtative Property of Addition to start with either addend.

$$3,928 + \mathbf{80} = 4,008$$
$$4,008 + \mathbf{400} = 4,408$$
$$4,408 + \mathbf{2,000} = 6,408$$

Use Compensation

Use the Identity Property of Addition to add and subtract the same number.

$$3,928 + 2,480 = (3,928 + 72) + (2,480 - 72)$$
$$= 4,000 + 2,408 = 6,408$$

Subtraction Strategies

Find 9,125 − 7,985 with mental math.

Count Up

$$7,985 + 15 = 8,000$$
$$8,000 + 125 = 8,125$$
$$8,125 + 1,000 = 9,125$$
Added 15 + 125 + 1,000 = 1,140

Count Down

$$9,125 - 25 = 9,100$$
$$9,100 - 60 = 9,040$$
$$9,040 - 900 = 8,140$$
$$8,140 - 7,000 = 1,140$$

Use Compensation

$$9,125 - 7,985$$
$$= (9,125 + 15) - (7,985 + 15)$$
$$= 9,140 - 8,000 = 1,140$$

For **1–10**, use mental math to solve.

1. 389 + 356

2. 611 − 189

3. 4,576 + 2,345

4. 7,300 − 4,126

5. 2,524 + 3,087 + 1,476

6. 8,843 − 7,645

7. 2,507 + 4,996

8. 1,700 − 398

9. 4,076 + 21,024

10. 11,219 − 1,219

11. **Precision** What is the difference between the speeds of the planets Venus and Mars? Explain how to use mental math to solve.

Speeds of Planets	
Planet	**Speed (miles per hour)**
Neptune	12,253
Saturn	21,637
Mars	53,979
Venus	78,341

12. Write the speed of the planet Saturn using number names.

13. Choose a mental math strategy, and find the difference between the speeds of the planets Neptune and Saturn.

14. Find 4,290 + 3,602. Explain how to use mental math to solve.

15. Mrs. Simms bought 10 cases of spaghetti noodles for the spaghetti dinner fund raiser. There are 8 boxes of spaghetti in each case. How many boxes of noodles did Mrs. Simms buy?

16. **Higher Order Thinking** See Guy's work. Is his answer correct? What mistake did he make?

Guy's Work

8,265 – 7,145

= (8,265 – 55) (7,145 + 55)

= 8,210 – 7,200

= 1,010

✓ **Assessment Practice**

17. Use mental math to find 1,484 + 1,210.

Ⓐ 2,694

Ⓑ 2,704

Ⓒ 2,784

Ⓓ 2,794

18. Use mental math to find 2,800 – 1,975.

Ⓐ 725

Ⓑ 775

Ⓒ 825

Ⓓ 875

Name _____

Another Look!

You can use rounding to estimate sums and differences.

When you have an exact answer to an addition or subtraction problem, you can use your estimate to determine whether your exact answer is reasonable.

To estimate 64,236 + 15,542:

Round to the nearest hundred
64,200 + 15,500 = 79,700

Round to the nearest thousand
64,000 + 16,000 = 80,000

Round to the nearest ten thousand
60,000 + 20,000 = 80,000

To estimate 452,776 − 186,257:

Round to the nearest thousand
453,000 − 186,000 = 267,000

Round to the nearest ten thousand
450,000 − 190,000 = 260,000

Round to the nearest hundred thousand
500,000 − 200,000 = 300,000

Leveled Practice For **1–10**, estimate each sum or difference.

1. 753,265 → ☐☐0,000
   − 419,057 → − ☐☐0,000

2. 48,765 → ☐☐,000
   + 9,221 → + ☐,000

3. 7,792 → ☐,000
   − 3,847 → − ☐,000

4. 2,189
   + 1,388

5. 9,245
   − 4,033

6. 1,000,000
   − 447,618

7. 65,327 − 14,231

8. 391,192 + 511,864

Your estimate may be different from someone else's estimate because you both round differently. That's okay.

9. 8,475 + 1,329

10. 812,910 − 709,085

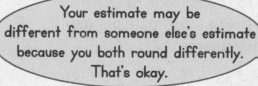

Ocean Area

Ocean	Area (sq km)
Arctic Ocean	14,090
Atlantic Ocean	82,400
Indian Ocean	65,527
Pacific Ocean	165,760

DATA

11. About how much greater is the area of the largest ocean than the area of the smallest ocean?

12. Write the area of the Pacific Ocean in expanded form.

13. Construct Arguments In a local election, 138,201 people voted for the winning candidate. If she won by 29,288 votes, about how many votes did the other candidate receive? Explain how to estimate.

14. In one weekend, a theater sells 74,877 tickets to a new movie. They sell 21,243 tickets the following week and 39,643 tickets the following weekend. About how many more tickets do they sell the first weekend than the following week and weekend combined?

15. Is 3,540 reasonable for the difference 9,760 − 5,220? Explain.

16. Higher Order Thinking The hospital hoped to raise $750,000 at a telethon. They raised $398,622 the first day and raised $379,873 the second day. Did the hospital reach their goal? Explain how you estimated.

☑ **Assessment Practice**

17. Pau's family drove 1,377 miles from Miami to Chicago. Then, they drove 1,350 miles from Chicago to Yellowstone National Park. Which is the best estimate of how many miles they drove in all?

Ⓐ 1,800 miles

Ⓑ 2,000 miles

Ⓒ 2,200 miles

Ⓓ 2,800 miles

18. There were 87,169 fans at the game on Saturday and only 37,245 fans at the game on Sunday. Which is a reasonable difference of 87,169 − 37,245? Use an estimate to decide.

Ⓐ 58,924 fans

Ⓑ 49,824 fans

Ⓒ 38,924 fans

Ⓓ 34,824 fans

Additional Practice 2-3
Add Whole Numbers

Another Look!

Add 137 + 145.

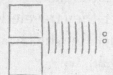

Step 1

Add ones.

7 ones + 5 ones = 12 ones

Regroup: 12 ones = 1 ten + 2 ones

$$\begin{array}{r} \overset{1}{1}37 \\ +145 \\ \hline 2 \end{array}$$

Step 2

Add tens.

3 tens + 4 tens + 1 ten = 8 tens

$$\begin{array}{r} \overset{1}{1}37 \\ +145 \\ \hline 82 \end{array}$$

Step 3

Add hundreds.

1 hundred + 1 hundred = 2 hundreds

$$\begin{array}{r} \overset{1}{1}37 \\ +145 \\ \hline 282 \end{array}$$

In **1–12**, find each sum.

1. $\begin{array}{r} 456 \\ +134 \\ \hline \end{array}$

2. $\begin{array}{r} 638 \\ +257 \\ \hline \end{array}$

3. $\begin{array}{r} 263 \\ +375 \\ \hline \end{array}$

4. $\begin{array}{r} 914 \\ +435 \\ \hline \end{array}$

5. $\begin{array}{r} 829 \\ +413 \\ \hline \end{array}$

6. $\begin{array}{r} 585 \\ +387 \\ \hline \end{array}$

7. $\begin{array}{r} 287 \\ +526 \\ \hline \end{array}$

8. $\begin{array}{r} 845 \\ +178 \\ \hline \end{array}$

9. $\begin{array}{r} 659 \\ +486 \\ \hline \end{array}$

10. $\begin{array}{r} 384 \\ +491 \\ \hline \end{array}$

11. $\begin{array}{r} 591 \\ +680 \\ \hline \end{array}$

12. $\begin{array}{r} 745 \\ +557 \\ \hline \end{array}$

The table shows the miles an under-12 soccer team travels to play teams in other cities. Use the table to answer **13–14**.

13. In October, the team traveled to Tampa and to Gainesville. How many miles did they drive in all?

City	Miles (round trip)
Daytona Beach	180
Gainesville	142
St. Augustine	82
Tallahassee	334
Tampa	396

DATA

14. Make Sense and Persevere In August, the team traveled to Tallahassee and St. Augustine. In September, they traveled to Gainesville and Daytona Beach. In which month did they travel farther? Explain.

15. How many times do you need to regroup to add 873 + 465? Explain.

16. Higher Order Thinking Explain how to find 398 + 257 with mental math and with the standard algorithm. Which do you think is easier? Why?

✓ **Assessment Practice**

17. Select all the correct sums.

☐ 646 + 259 = 895

☐ 828 + 147 = 975

☐ 295 + 768 = 1,063

☐ 388 + 375 = 753

☐ 952 + 484 = 1,436

18. Which is the missing addend?

556 + _____ = 1,046

Ⓐ 510

Ⓑ 480

Ⓒ 490

Ⓓ 523

Name _____

Another Look!

You can add two or more numbers when you line up the numbers by place value. Add one place at a time.

Find 3,456 + 2,139 + 5,547.

Estimate: 3,000 + 2,000 + 6,000 = 11,000

Step 1

Line up the numbers by place value.

Add the ones.

Regroup if needed.

$$
\begin{array}{r}
\overset{2}{3,45}6 \\
2,139 \\
+\ 5,547 \\
\hline
2
\end{array}
$$

Regroup 22 ones as 2 tens and 2 ones.

Step 2

Add the tens and hundreds.

Regroup if needed.

$$
\begin{array}{r}
\overset{1}{} \overset{1}{} \overset{2}{}\ \\
3,456 \\
2,139 \\
+\ 5,547 \\
\hline
142
\end{array}
$$

Keep digits in columns as you add.

Step 3

Add the thousands.

Regroup for ten thousands if necessary.

$$
\begin{array}{r}
\overset{1}{} \overset{1}{} \overset{2}{}\ \\
3,456 \\
2,139 \\
+\ 5,547 \\
\hline
11,142
\end{array}
$$

11,142 is reasonable because it is close to the estimate of 11,000.

For **1–8**, estimate, and then find each sum.

To check if your answer is reasonable, see if it is close to your estimate.

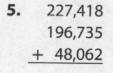

1.
$$
\begin{array}{r}
9,945 \\
+\ 3,343 \\
\hline
\end{array}
$$

2.
$$
\begin{array}{r}
12,566 \\
+\ 5,532 \\
\hline
\end{array}
$$

3.
$$
\begin{array}{r}
387,969 \\
+\ 562,031 \\
\hline
\end{array}
$$

4.
$$
\begin{array}{r}
629,979 \\
294,116 \\
+\ 75,905 \\
\hline
\end{array}
$$

5.
$$
\begin{array}{r}
227,418 \\
196,735 \\
+\ 48,062 \\
\hline
\end{array}
$$

6.
$$
\begin{array}{r}
82,011 \\
96,489 \\
+\ 76,988 \\
\hline
\end{array}
$$

7.
$$
\begin{array}{r}
126,267 \\
15,809 \\
+\ 8,764 \\
\hline
\end{array}
$$

8.
$$
\begin{array}{r}
45,101 \\
35,099 \\
+\ 10,000 \\
\hline
\end{array}
$$

9. **Number Sense** Estimate then add to find the combined length of the four highways shown in the table. Is your answer reasonable? Explain.

Lengths of Interstate Highways	
Interstate	Length (miles)
I-90	3,102
I-10	2,460
I-70	2,153
I-80	2,899

10. Highway I-10 is having an extension added on. It will then be 3,000 miles long. How long is the extension?

11. A shipping company delivered 38,728 letters and 41,584 packages. How many total items did the company deliver?

12. The Fatigato family has two cars. One cost $38,295. The other car cost $33,187. Which car cost more? Write a comparison.

13. **Higher Order Thinking** Leona added 206,425 + 128,579 + 314,004. Should Leona's sum be greater or less than 660,000? Explain.

14. In one week, Katy walks 1,750 meters and runs 1,925 meters. How many meters does Katy walk and run?

✓ Assessment Practice

15. Select all the correct sums.

☐ 6,384 + 5,649 = 11,923

☐ 8,762 + 15,409 = 24,171

☐ 39,719 + 27,662 = 67,381

☐ 74,982 + 125,637 = 200,519

☐ 117,875 + 19,794 = 137,669

16. Find the sum.

$$\begin{array}{r} 87,462 \\ + 19,750 \\ \hline \end{array}$$

Ⓐ 106,112

Ⓑ 106,212

Ⓒ 107,912

Ⓓ 107,212

Name _____

Additional Practice 2-5
Subtract Whole Numbers

Another Look!

Subtract 274 −149.

Step 1

Subtract ones.

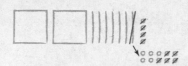

Regroup: 7 tens + 4 ones =
6 tens + 14 ones

14 ones − 9 ones = 5 ones

$$\begin{array}{r} {}^{6\ 14} \\ 2\cancel{7}\cancel{4} \\ -\ 149 \\ \hline 5 \end{array}$$

Step 2

Subtract tens.

6 tens − 4 tens = 2 tens

$$\begin{array}{r} {}^{6\ 14} \\ 2\cancel{7}\cancel{4} \\ -\ 149 \\ \hline 25 \end{array}$$

Step 3

Subtract hundreds.

2 hundreds − 1 hundred =
1 hundred

$$\begin{array}{r} {}^{6\ 14} \\ 2\cancel{7}\cancel{4} \\ -\ 149 \\ \hline 125 \end{array}$$

In **1–9**, subtract. Check that your answer is reasonable.

Estimate the difference first. Your answer is reasonable if it is close to the estimate.

1. 376
   − 234

2. 538
   − 267

3. 643
   − 329

4. 814
   − 475

5. 762
   − 583

6. 975
   − 788

7. 212
   − 89

8. 845
   − 675

9. 411
   − 123

According to the Florida Fish and Wildlife Conservation Commission, a boat may harvest a maximum of 250 spiny lobsters per day. The table shows the number of lobsters harvested by a boat in 4 days. Use the table to answer 10–11.

10. How many more lobsters did the boat harvest on day 1 than day 4? Explain how to estimate to check that your answer is reasonable.

DATA	Day	Number of Lobsters
	1	176
	2	215
	3	96
	4	117

11. How many more lobsters did the boat harvest on days 1 and 4 combined than on day 2? Explain.

12. When subtracting 537 − 443, why is there no digit in hundreds place?

13. **Higher Order Thinking** How many times do you need to regroup to subtract 847 − 268? How do you know?

14. What is the difference?

$$
\begin{array}{r}
851 \\
-\ 374 \\
\end{array}
$$

Ⓐ 577

Ⓑ 483

Ⓒ 477

Ⓓ 473

15. What is the missing digit in the subtraction statement?

5	7	8	9

$$
\begin{array}{r}
5\ 2\ 6 \\
-\ 3\ \square\ 7 \\
\hline
1\ 3\ 9 \\
\end{array}
$$

Practice Video Tools Games

Additional Practice 2-6
Subtract Greater Numbers

Another Look!

To subtract whole numbers with the standard algorithm, subtract each place. Start with ones and regroup when necessary.

Find 7,445 − 1,368.

Estimate: 7,000 − 1,000 = 6,000

Step 1	Step 2	Step 3	Step 4

Step 1

$$\begin{array}{r} 7,4\overset{3\ 15}{4\cancel{5}} \\ -\ 1,368 \\ \hline 7 \end{array}$$

Regroup: 4 tens
5 ones = 3 tens
15 ones

Subtract 8 ones from 15 ones.

Step 2

$$\begin{array}{r} 7,\overset{13}{\overset{3\ 3\ 15}{4\cancel{4}\cancel{5}}} \\ -\ 1,368 \\ \hline 77 \end{array}$$

Regroup: 4 hundreds
3 tens = 3 hundreds
13 tens

Subtract 6 tens from 13 tens.

Step 3

$$\begin{array}{r} 7,\overset{13}{\overset{3\ 3\ 15}{4\cancel{4}\cancel{5}}} \\ -\ 1,368 \\ \hline 077 \end{array}$$

Subtract 3 hundreds from 3 hundreds.

Step 4

$$\begin{array}{r} 7,\overset{13}{\overset{3\ 3\ 15}{4\cancel{4}\cancel{5}}} \\ -\ 1,368 \\ \hline 6,077 \end{array}$$

Subtract 1 thousand from 7 thousands.

Check for reasonableness: The difference 6,077 is reasonable because it is close to the estimate of 6,000.

For **1–8**, find the difference. Estimate to check if your answer is reasonable.

1. $\begin{array}{r} 8,737 \\ -\ 6,754 \\ \hline \end{array}$

2. $\begin{array}{r} 411,765 \\ -\ 402,120 \\ \hline \end{array}$

3. $\begin{array}{r} 43,429 \\ -\ 17,101 \\ \hline \end{array}$

4. $\begin{array}{r} 952,746 \\ -\ 184,524 \\ \hline \end{array}$

5. $\begin{array}{r} 17,863 \\ -\ 3,747 \\ \hline \end{array}$

6. $\begin{array}{r} 513,363 \\ -\ 382,895 \\ \hline \end{array}$

7. $\begin{array}{r} 4,226 \\ -\ 2,958 \\ \hline \end{array}$

8. $\begin{array}{r} 67,451 \\ -\ 29,609 \\ \hline \end{array}$

9. The Environmental Club's goal is to collect 9,525 cans by the end of four months. How can you find the number of cans the club needs to collect in September to meet their goal? How many more cans do they need?

Month	Cans Collected
June	1,898
July	2,643
August	2,287

10. Naima's pedometer recorded 43,498 steps in one week. Her goal is 88,942 steps. How many more steps does Naima need to reach her goal?

11. **Critique Reasoning** Mitch wrote the subtraction below. What mistake did Mitch make? What is the correct answer?

$$\begin{array}{r} 657,392 \\ - \ 434,597 \\ \hline 222,895 \end{array}$$

12. Compare the values of the 2s and 5s in 55,220.

13. **Higher Order Thinking** Find 542 − 399 using the standard algorithm and another method. Which method do you prefer? Explain why.

✓ **Assessment Practice**

14. What is the missing digit in the subtraction statement?

$$\begin{array}{r} 8,2\ 5\ 4 \\ - \ 3,\square\ 7\ 6 \\ \hline 4,6\ 7\ 8 \end{array}$$

Ⓐ 4   Ⓒ 6

Ⓑ 5   Ⓓ 7

15. What is the difference 25,348 − 12,564?

Ⓐ 12,748

Ⓑ 12,784

Ⓒ 12,224

Ⓓ 2,784

Practice Video Tools Games

Another Look!

Find 700,402 − 297,354.

Estimate: 700,000 − 300,000 = 400,000

Step 1	**Step 2**	**Step 3**	**Step 4**
Regroup	**Subtract**	**Regroup**	**Subtract**
$\begin{array}{r} \overset{3\,10\,12}{700,40\cancel{2}} \\ -\ 297,354 \\ \hline \end{array}$	$\begin{array}{r} \overset{3\,10\,12}{700,40\cancel{2}} \\ -\ 297,354 \\ \hline 048 \end{array}$	$\begin{array}{r} \overset{6\,10\,10\ \ 3\,10\,12}{700,402} \\ -\ 297,354 \\ \hline 048 \end{array}$	$\begin{array}{r} \overset{6\,10\,10\ \ 3\,10\,12}{700,402} \\ -\ 297,354 \\ \hline 403,048 \end{array}$
4 hundreds = 3 hundreds + 10 tens 10 tens + 2 ones = 9 tens + 12 ones	12 − 4 = 8 ones 90 − 50 = 40 = 4 tens 300 − 300 = 0 hundreds	7 hundred thousands = 6 hundred thousands + 10 ten thousands 10 ten thousands = 9 ten thousands + 10 thousands	10,000 − 7,000 = 3 thousands 90,000 − 90,000 = 0 ten thousands 600,000 − 200,000 = 4 hundred thousands

> The difference 403,048 is reasonable because it is close to the estimate of 400,000.

For 1–12, subtract.

1. $\begin{array}{r} 61,070 \\ -\ \ \ 4,981 \\ \hline \end{array}$

2. $\begin{array}{r} 5,000 \\ -\ 2,058 \\ \hline \end{array}$

3. $\begin{array}{r} 815,950 \\ -\ 423,147 \\ \hline \end{array}$

4. $\begin{array}{r} 90,800 \\ -\ 37,638 \\ \hline \end{array}$

5. $\begin{array}{r} 102,604 \\ -\ \ \ \ 6,174 \\ \hline \end{array}$

6. $\begin{array}{r} 22,700 \\ -\ 20,487 \\ \hline \end{array}$

7. $\begin{array}{r} 40,000 \\ -\ 29,526 \\ \hline \end{array}$

8. $\begin{array}{r} 600,470 \\ -\ 307,299 \\ \hline \end{array}$

9. 8,106 − 2,999

10. 214,507 − 83,569

11. 10,400 − 6,392

12. 45,500 − 9,450

13. Este subtracts 9,405 from 11,000 and gets 3,595. Is Este's answer reasonable? Explain.

14. A park district holds a fundraiser over 4 weekends in which teams swim laps for donations. The park district's goal is 40,000 laps. Over three weekends the teams swam 8,597 laps, 11,065 laps, and 9,211 laps. How many laps do they need to swim the fourth weekend to reach their goal?

15. There are 332,054 people in a city. 168,278 are under the age of eighteen. How many people are eighteen or older?

16. Higher Order Thinking Blaine subtracted 342,139 from 601,800. Is Blaine's answer correct? If not, explain why, and write the correct answer.

$$\begin{array}{r} 601,800 \\ - 342,139 \\ \hline 359,661 \end{array}$$

17. How much longer is the Amazon River than the Lower Tunguska and Ganges Rivers combined? Explain.

DATA	World Rivers	
	River	Length (kilometers)
	Nile	6,650
	Lower Tunguska	2,989
	Senegal	1,641
	Ganges	2,620
	Amazon	6,400

✓ **Assessment Practice**

18. Select all the correct differences.

- ☐ $7,000 - 4,238 = 2,762$
- ☐ $20,400 - 9,280 = 10,120$
- ☐ $72,004 - 28,376 = 43,628$
- ☐ $82,000 - 47,154 = 34,846$
- ☐ $500,098 - 275,329 = 225,769$

19. Find the difference.

$$\begin{array}{r} 9,000 \\ - 2,942 \\ \hline \end{array}$$

- Ⓐ 6,058
- Ⓑ 6,062
- Ⓒ 6,158
- Ⓓ 11,942

Practice   Video   Tools   Games

Additional Practice 2-8
Reasoning

Another Look!

In a week, a farmer collected 3,978 red apples and 2,504 green apples. He sold a total of 4,856 apples. He took the rest of the apples to the Farmer's Market. How many apples did the farmer have left for the Farmer's Market?

Tell how you can use quantitative reasoning to find the answer.

- I can identify the quantities given.

- I can draw diagrams to show relationships.

- I can give the answer using the correct unit.

> When you use reasoning, you show how quantities are related.

Identify quantities and the relationships between them to solve.

First find a, the number of apples the farmer collected.

a apples	
3,978	2,504

$3,978 + 2,504 = 6,482$

The farmer collected 6,482 apples.

Then find m, the number of apples left for the Farmer's Market.

6,482	
4,856	m

$6,482 - 4,856 = 1,626$

1,626 apples were left.

Reasoning

A census said that there were 659,000 French Creole speakers in the United States. There were 186,000 more Arabic speakers than French Creole speakers. How many Arabic speakers were there? Use Exercises 1–2 to answer the question.

1. What quantities are given in the problem, and what do the numbers mean?

2. What is the relationship between the quantities? Complete the bar diagram to find a, the number of Arabic speakers. Write and solve an equation.

a

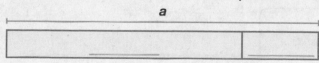

Music

The table shows how many times a song was downloaded the first four days it was on sale. How many more times was it downloaded on days 1 and 2 combined than on days 3 and 4 combined?

DATA

Day	Times Downloaded
1	98,273
2	313,280
3	106,548
4	270,463

3. **Reasoning** What quantities are given in the problem and what do the numbers mean?

When you use reasoning, you identify the quantities given and their relationships.

4. **Make Sense and Persevere** What strategy can you use to solve the problem?

5. **Model with Math** Complete the bar diagrams to show how to represent the hidden questions. Then, write and solve equations.

6. **Model with Math** How many more times was the song downloaded on days 1 and 2 combined than on days 3 and 4 combined? Complete the bar diagram and write and solve an equation to find the difference, *d*.

t = total days 1 and 2

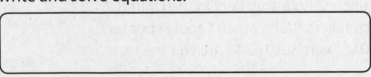

s = total days 3 and 4

Practice Video Tools Games

Another Look!

Use basic facts and either place value or the Associative Property of Multiplication to multiply by multiples of 10, 100, and 1,000.

$3 \times 70 = 3 \times 7$ tens
$\qquad = 21$ tens
$\qquad = 210$

$3 \times 700 = 3 \times 7$ hundreds
$\qquad = 21$ hundreds
$\qquad = 2,100$

$3 \times 7,000 = 3 \times 7$ thousands
$\qquad = 21$ thousands
$\qquad = 21,000$

$9 \times 50 = 9 \times (5 \times 10)$
$\qquad = (9 \times 5) \times 10$
$\qquad = 45 \times 10$
$\qquad = 450$

$9 \times 500 = 9 \times (5 \times 100)$
$\qquad = (9 \times 5) \times 100$
$\qquad = 45 \times 100$
$\qquad = 4,500$

$9 \times 5,000 = 9 \times (5 \times 1,000)$
$\qquad = (9 \times 5) \times 1,000$
$\qquad = 45 \times 1,000$
$\qquad = 45,000$

For **1–18**, find each product.

1. $8 \times 20 =$ _____
$8 \times 200 =$ _____
$8 \times 2,000 =$ _____

2. $9 \times 40 =$ _____
$9 \times 400 =$ _____
$9 \times 4,000 =$ _____

3. $3 \times 90 =$ _____
$3 \times 900 =$ _____
$3 \times 9,000 =$ _____

4. $7 \times 60 =$ _____
$7 \times 600 =$ _____
$7 \times 6,000 =$ _____

5. $5 \times 70 =$ _____
$5 \times 700 =$ _____
$5 \times 7,000 =$ _____

6. $2 \times 40 =$ _____
$2 \times 400 =$ _____
$2 \times 4,000 =$ _____

7. 3×40

8. $3,000 \times 9$

9. 80×3

10. $8,000 \times 5$

11. $8 \times 7,000$

12. 2×90

13. $3,000 \times 4$

14. $7 \times 6,000$

15. $5,000 \times 6$

16. 2×800

17. 90×8

18. $3,000 \times 6$

19. Adele has 6 sheets of stickers. Bea has 3 sheets of the same stickers. How many stickers do they have altogether?

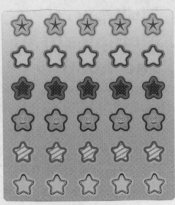

20. Algebra There were 4 times the number of students in fourth grade at the basketball game. How many students, *s*, attended the basketball game? Write and solve an equation.

School Population	
Grade	Number of Students
Fourth Grade	50
Fifth Grade	54
Sixth Grade	60

21. Jenna saved $100. She wants to buy 6 games that cost $20 each. Does Jenna have enough money? Explain.

t total cost of games

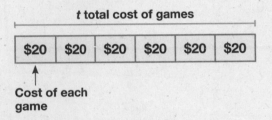

| $20 | $20 | $20 | $20 | $20 | $20 |

↑
Cost of each game

22. Higher Order Thinking Mr. Young has 30 times as many pencils as Jack. The whole school has 200 times as many pencils as Jack. If Jack has 2 pencils, how many pencils does Mr. Young have? How many more pencils does the whole school have than Mr. Young?

☑ **Assessment Practice**

23. How many zeros will be in the product of 7 × 5,000?

A.

Without calculating the answer, explain how to use the Associative Property to find the number of zeros in the product.

B.

Without calculating an answer, explain how to use place-value strategies to find the number of zeros in the product.

Name _____

Another Look!

To estimate, you can round 3-digit numbers to the nearest hundred and round 4-digit numbers to the nearest thousand.

Use rounding to estimate 7 × 215.

First, round 215 to the nearest hundred.

```
        215
<———————|————|————|———————>
  200        250        300
```

215 rounds to 200.

Then, multiply. 7 × 200 = 1,400

So, 7 × 215 is about 1,400.

Check if 2,885 × 4 = 11,540 is reasonable.

First round 2,885 to the nearest thousand. 2,885 rounds to 3,000.

Then, multiply.
3,000 × 4 = 12,000

So, 2,885 × 4 is about 12,000.

11,540 is a reasonable answer.

For 1–6, estimate the product.

1. 4 × 279

⬇ Round 279 to _____.

4 × _____ = _____

2. 9 × 4,720

⬇ Round 4,720 to _____.

9 × _____ = _____

3. 8 × 89

⬇ Round 89 to _____.

8 × _____ = _____

4. 183 × 4

5. 3 × 1,675

6. 8,210 × 2

For 7–9, estimate to check if the answer is reasonable.

7. 8 × 578 = 4,624

⬇ Round 578 to _____.

8 × _____ = _____

Reasonable   Not Reasonable

8. 3 × 8,230 = 2,469

⬇ Round 8,230 to _____.

3 × _____ = _____

Reasonable   Not Reasonable

9. 7 × 289 = 2,023

⬇ Round 289 to _____.

7 × _____ = _____

Reasonable   Not Reasonable

10. **A-Z** **Vocabulary** Use *expanded form* or *number name* to complete the definition.

A number written as the sum of the value of its digits is written in _____.

11. **enVision®** STEM The Ojos del Salado volcano has an elevation about 3 times as great as the Khangar volcano. If the Khangar volcano is 6,562 feet above sea level, what is the approximate elevation of the Ojos del Salado volcano?

For **12–13**, use the graph at the right.

12. **Number Sense** Estimate how many of Part B would be made in 3 months.

13. It costs the factory $4 to make each Part A. About how much does it cost to make Part A each month?

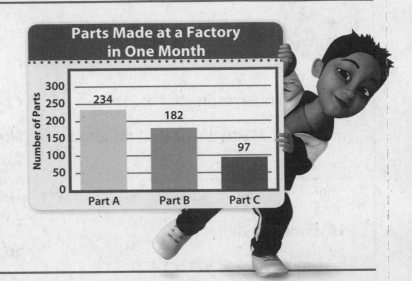

Parts Made at a Factory in One Month

---

14. **Higher Order Thinking** A Deluxe Package costs $50 and includes one of each of the individual pictures listed in the table. Estimate about how much money you save with the Deluxe Package instead of buying one of each of the individual pictures. Explain.

DATA

Individual Picture Prices

Picture Size	Price
8 × 10	$18
5 × 7	$14
4 × 6	$10
8 wallets	$18

---

15. Shawn found it took him 429 steps to get from home to the outside basketball court. How many steps does it take to make 8 one-way trips? Choose the best estimate.

 Ⓐ About 400 steps

 Ⓑ About 3,200 steps

 Ⓒ About 3,400 steps

 Ⓓ About 4,000 steps

16. A city recycles 7,612 pounds of newspaper one year. If they recycle the same amount each year, about how many pounds would be recycled in 7 years? Choose the best estimate.

 Ⓐ About 4,900 pounds

 Ⓑ About 49,000 pounds

 Ⓒ About 56,000 pounds

 Ⓓ About 76,000 pounds

Name _____

Practice   Video   Tools   Games

Additional Practice 3-3
Use Arrays and Partial Products to Multiply

Another Look!

The partial products are modeled by the drawing.

Find 3 × 124.   3 × 124 is about 3 × 100 = 300.

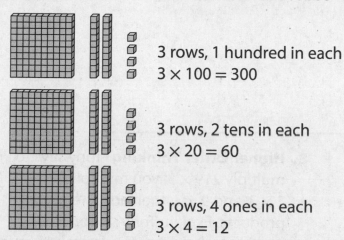

3 rows, 1 hundred in each
3 × 100 = 300

3 rows, 2 tens in each
3 × 20 = 60

3 rows, 4 ones in each
3 × 4 = 12

```
   124
 ×   3
  ----
    12
    60
 + 300
  ----
   372
```

For **1–4**, multiply. Use place-value blocks or draw arrays as needed.

1. 2 × 411

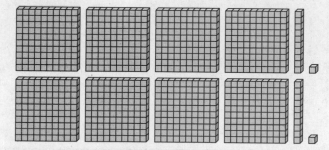

2 rows, 4 hundreds in each
2 × _____ = _____

2 rows, 1 ten in each
2 × _____ = _____

2 rows, 1 one in each
2 × _____ = _____

_____ + _____ + _____ = _____

2. 3 × 316

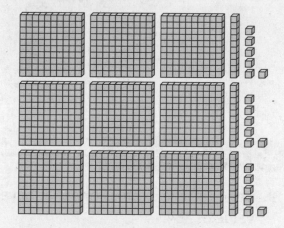

3 rows, 3 hundreds in each
3 × _____ = _____

3 rows, 1 ten in each
3 × _____ = _____

3 rows, 6 ones in each
3 × _____ = _____

_____ + _____ + _____ = _____

3. 5 × 178

4. 4 × 213

5. How many marbles are in 4 large bags and 7 small bags?

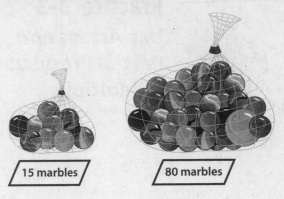

15 marbles   80 marbles

6. Use Appropriate Tools Show how you can use place-value blocks or draw an array to find the partial products for 4×125.

---

7. A red tree frog can jump up to 150 times its body length. How far can this tree frog jump?

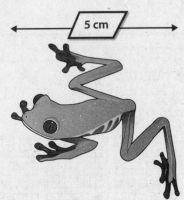

5 cm

8. Higher Order Thinking Tony says to multiply 219×3, you multiply 2×3, 1×3, and 9×3, then add the partial products. Explain Tony's error. How would you help Tony understand how to correctly multiply 219×3?

✓ **Assessment Practice**

9. Select all the expressions that have a value of 464.

☐ 400×64

☐ $(4 \times 100) + 16$

☐ 4×116

☐ $4 \times (400 + 60 + 4)$

☐ $(4 \times 100) + (4 \times 10) + (4 \times 6)$

10. Which are correct partial products for 73×8?

Ⓐ 240, 56

Ⓑ 56, 24

Ⓒ 480, 24

Ⓓ 24, 560

Name _____

Another Look!

The city board wants to build a new fountain for a downtown park. They agree to set aside an area that is 7 yards wide and 14 yards long. What is the area for the new fountain?

> Area models and partial products are useful tools to solve multiplication problems.

	10	4
7	7 × 10	7 × 4

Estimate: 7 × 14 is about 7 × 10 = 70.

7 × 10 = 70   7 × 4 = 728

70 + 28 = 98

$$\begin{array}{r} 14 \\ \times\ 7 \\ \hline 28 \\ +70 \\ \hline 98 \end{array}$$ 7 × 4 ones
7 × 1 ten

The area for the new fountain is 98 square yards.

The product, 98, is close to the estimate of 70. The answer is reasonable.

For **1–4**, use the area model and partial products.

1.

	40	6
8		

$$\begin{array}{r} 46 \\ \times\ 8 \end{array}$$

2.

	70	9
3		

$$\begin{array}{r} 79 \\ \times\ 3 \end{array}$$

3.

	800	90	5
9			

$$\begin{array}{r} 895 \\ \times\ 9 \end{array}$$

4.

	600	50	1
6			

$$\begin{array}{r} 651 \\ \times\ 6 \end{array}$$

5. Use the Distributive Property and partial products to find 5×727.

6. A lodge at a state park has 49 rooms. Up to five people may stay in each room. What is the maximum number of people who can stay at the lodge at one time?

7. Lauren read 36 books during the year. If she reads the same number of books for 6 years in a row, how many total books will Lauren read?

8. A parking garage has 8 levels. Each level has parking spaces for 78 cars. How many cars can park in the garage at one time?

For **9–10**, use the table at the right.

9. A banquet room is being set up for a party using round tables. How many chairs are used for the round tables?

10. Higher Order Thinking Which of the three table types allows seating for the greatest number of people? Explain.

Hotel Banquet Room Plans		
Type of Table	**Number of Tables**	**Chairs that Fit Around Each**
Long Dining Tables	62	8
Round Dining Tables	105	6
Square Dining Tables	150	4

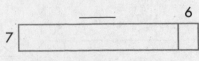 **Assessment Practice**

11. What is the missing factor?

$7 \times ? = 392$

Ⓐ 50
Ⓑ 66
Ⓒ 56
Ⓓ 60

12. Which are the partial products for this area model?

5×385

Ⓐ 25, 440, 1,500
Ⓑ 15,000, 400, 25
Ⓒ 25, 400, 1,500
Ⓓ 1,500, 40, 56

Name _____

Another Look!

Three groups of 1,245 students attended the concert. How many students attended the concert?

Find 3 × 1,245.

You can use area models and partial products to find the products of greater numbers.

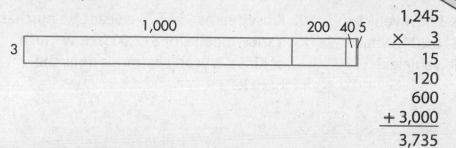

```
      1,000              200 40 5
  3 |                          |
```

$$
\begin{array}{r}
1,245 \\
\times\quad 3 \\
\hline
15 \\
120 \\
600 \\
+\,3,000 \\
\hline
3,735
\end{array}
$$

3,735 students attended the concert.

For **1–6**, multiply. Use the area model and partial products.

1.
$$
\begin{array}{r}
6317 \\
\times\quad 9 \\
\end{array}
$$

```
         6,000         300 7
  9 |                      |
                           10
```

2.
$$
\begin{array}{r}
3,933 \\
\times\quad 4 \\
\end{array}
$$

```
         3,000         900 3
  4 |                     |
                          30
```

3.
$$
\begin{array}{r}
1,619 \\
\times\quad 7 \\
\end{array}
$$

```
         1,000         600 9
  7 |                      |
                           10
```

4.
$$
\begin{array}{r}
4,265 \\
\times\quad 5 \\
\end{array}
$$

```
         4,000         200 5
  5 |                     |
                          60
```

5.
$$
\begin{array}{r}
2,111 \\
\times\quad 5 \\
\end{array}
$$

```
         2,000         100 1
  5 |                     |
                          10
```

6.
$$
\begin{array}{r}
4,231 \\
\times\quad 2 \\
\end{array}
$$

```
         4,000         200 1
  2 |                     |
                          30
```

7. **Use Appropriate Tools** Complete the area model to find the product of 7 and 3,412.

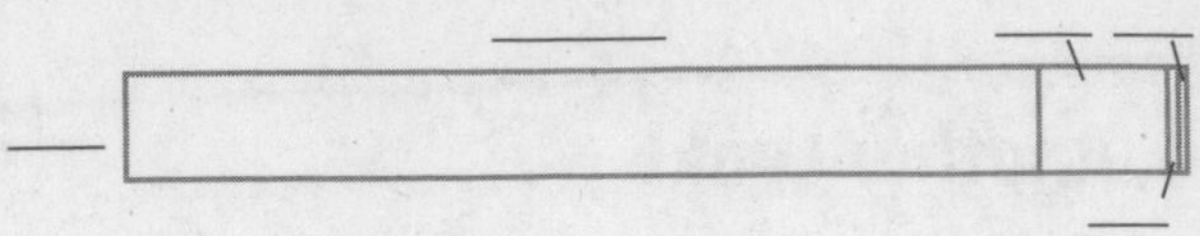

8. Fred's Auto Sales purchases 3 new vehicles for $11,219, $31,611, and $18,204. What was the total cost for all the vehicles?

9. Kinsey earns $54,625 a year. She purchases a snowmobile for $12,005. How much of Kinsey's yearly earnings does she have left?

10. **Number Sense** Dalton added 3,402 + 4,950 to get 8,352. Estimate the sum by rounding the addends to the nearest hundred. Is Dalton's sum reasonable? Explain.

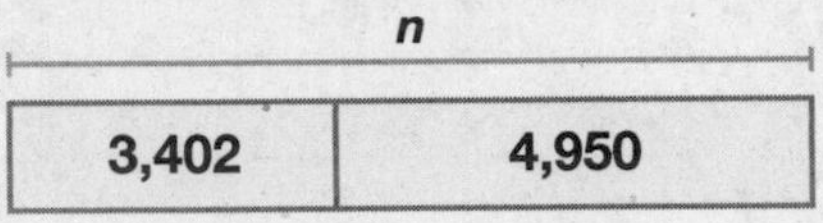

n	
3,402	4,950

11. **Higher Order Thinking** Josh used an algorithm to find the product for 9 × 239. His work is shown below. Is Josh's work correct? Explain.

```
    239
  ×   9
  1,800
    270
  +  81
  2,151
```

☑ **Assessment Practice**

12. Select all the numbers that are partial products of 8 × 1,126.

☐ 48

☐ 80

☐ 160

☐ 800

☐ 8,000

13. Which products have 240 as a partial product?

☐ 3 × 3,388

☐ 8 × 2,612

☐ 4 × 5,376

☐ 6 × 4,345

☐ 3 × 6,828

Practice Video Tools Games

Another Look!

Use mental math to calculate $4 \times 4,002$ and 8×60.

You can break numbers apart, use properties of operations, or use compensation to multiply mentally.

Use compensation to find $4 \times 3,998$.

4,000 is close to 3,998.
$4 \times 4,000 = 16,000$
$4,000 - 2 = 3,998$ $4 \times 2 = 8$
$16,000 - 8 = 15,992$

Use properties of operations to find 8×250.

$8 \times 250 = (2 \times 4) \times 250$
$= 2 \times (4 \times 250)$
$= 2 \times 1,000$
$= 2,000$

For **1–18**, multiply mentally to find each product. Explain which strategy you used.

1. $5 \times 395 = 5 \times ($ _____ $-$ _____ $)$

2. $7 \times 3,012 = 7 \times ($ _____ $+$ _____ $)$

3. 9×898

4. 2×144

5. 4×408

6. 8×15

7. 36×9

8. 3×496

9. 4×509

10. $3,004 \times 6$

11. 6×198

12. 5×999

13. 6×250

14. 4×525

15. 6×28

16. 7×156

17. $9 \times 1,276$

18. $3 \times 1,607$

For **19–20**, use the picture at the right:

19. **Reasoning** The longest blue whale on record was about 18 scuba divers in length. Use breaking apart to estimate the length of the blue whale.

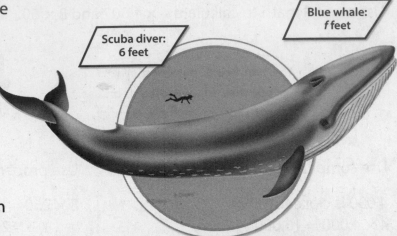

Scuba diver:
6 feet

Blue whale:
f feet

20. Explain how to estimate the length of the whale using compensation.

---

21. In an election, 589,067 people voted. Write 589,067 in expanded form and using number names.

22. **Higher Order Thinking** Davidson's Bakery bakes 108 cookies and 96 muffins every hour. How many baked goods are baked in 4 hours? Use mental math to solve.

✓ Assessment Practice

23. Select all of the expressions that show how to use mental math to find the product of 8 × 490.

- ☐ 8 + (400 × 90)
- ☐ (8 × 400) + (8 × 90)
- ☐ (8 × 400) + (8 × 9)
- ☐ (8 × 500) − (8 × 10)
- ☐ 8 × (500 × 10)

24. Select all of the expressions that show how to use mental math to find the product of 4 × 2,025.

- ☐ 4 × (2,000 + 20 + 5)
- ☐ (4 × 2,000) + 25
- ☐ (4 × 2,000) + (4 × 25)
- ☐ 4 × (2,000 + 25)
- ☐ (4 × 2,000 × 25)

Practice   Video   Tools   Games

Another Look!

Additional Practice 3-7
Choose a Strategy to Multiply

Find 4 × 5,990.

Estimate: 5,990 is close to 6,000, so the product is close to 4 × 6,000 = 24,000.

One way to solve is to use partial products. You can create an area model, a place-value model, or use the Distributive Property of Multiplication.

```
          5,000              900  90
  4 [                        |    | ]
```

$4 \times 5{,}990 = 4 \times (5{,}000 + 900 + 90)$
$= (4 \times 5{,}000) + (4 \times 900) + (4 \times 90)$
$= 20{,}000 + 3{,}600 + 360$
$= 23{,}960$

Another way to solve is by compensation. Find 4 × 6,000 and then adjust the answer by subtracting the product of 4 and 10.

$5{,}990 = 6{,}000 - 10$
$4 \times 6{,}000 = 24{,}000$
$4 \times 10 = 40$
$4 \times 5{,}990 = 24{,}000 - 40$
$= 23{,}960$

The product 23,960 is reasonable because it is close to the estimate of 24,000.

For **1–15**, estimate. Then find each product by choosing an appropriate strategy.

Use your estimate to determine if your answer is reasonable.

1.	538	2.	214	3.	3,721
	× 4		× 8		× 7

4.	7,956	5.	92	6.	37
	× 8		× 4		× 8

7. 6 × 505   **8.** 3 × 589   **9.** 5 × 6,384

10. 2 × 9,497   **11.** 7 × 3,218   **12.** 9 × 1,938

13. 5,219 × 3   **14.** 6,205 × 3   **15.** 1,236 × 8

16. A grocery store orders 47 bags of onions and 162 bags of potatoes. The onions cost $2 per bag, and the potatoes cost $3 per bag. How much is spent on onions and potatoes?

17. The animal shelter charges $119 to adopt a pet. On Saturday, 2 dogs and 7 cats were adopted. How much money did the animal shelter receive from those adoptions?

18. Algebra The insect exhibit at the museum has 8 display cases with 417 insects in each case. Write and solve an equation to show how many insects, c, are displayed at the museum.

19. Kamiko and her 4 sisters each have 18 grandchildren. Calculate the total number of grandchildren of Kamiko and her 4 sisters.

20. Over the weekend, 1,719 tickets were sold for a musical. How much money did the musical bring in?

$3 each

21. Higher Order Thinking Bo has 23 video games for sale. He plans to donate the money he makes from each sale to a local charity. What is the least amount of money in whole dollars Bo should charge for each game in order to raise $100? Explain.

✓ **Assessment Practice**

22. Zoe has 1,500 beads. She wants to make 6 friendship bracelets. She needs 215 beads for each bracelet. How many beads will Zoe have left after making all 6 of the bracelets? Write equations to show how you solved the problem. Tell what your variables represent.

In a multi-step problem, look back to be sure you answered the question asked.

Name _____

Another Look!

A hardware store ordered 4 packs of large screws and 5 packs of smaller screws from a supplier. Each pack contains 150 screws. How many screws did the store order?

Tell how you can model with math.

- I can use bar diagrams and equations to represent and solve this problem.
- I can use previously learned concepts and skills.

> When you model with math, you use pictures and equations to show how the quantities in the problem are related.

Draw a bar diagram and write an equation to solve.

$4 + 5 = 9$ packs

$9 \times 150 = s$

$s = 1,350$

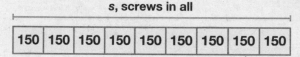

s, screws in all

| 150 | 150 | 150 | 150 | 150 | 150 | 150 | 150 | 150 |

↑ screws in one pack

The store ordered 1,350 screws.

Model with Math

When Mary was born, she weighed 8 pounds. When she was 10 years old, she weighed 10 times as much. How much more did Mary weigh when she was 10 years old than when she was born? Use Exercises 1–2 to answer the question.

1. Draw a picture, write and solve an equation to find Mary's weight, w, when she was 10 years old.

2. Draw a picture, and write and solve an equation to find the difference, d, between Mary's weight when she was 10 years old and when she was born.

School Supplies
A bookstore ordered 1,528 packs of pens and
1,823 packs of pencils at the prices shown. How
much did the bookstore spend on pens?

$3 per pack

$4 per pack

3. **Make Sense and Persevere** Have you seen a problem like
   this before? Explain.

4. **Reasoning** What do the numbers that you need to use in the
   problem mean?

5. **Model with Math** What operation can you use to solve the
   problem? Draw a bar diagram to show the operation.

   When you model with
   math, you use math
   you already know to
   solve a problem.

6. **Use Appropriate Tools** Would place-value blocks be a good
   tool to use to solve the problem? Explain.

7. **Be Precise** What was the total cost of the pens? Show
   that you computed accurately.

8. **Reasoning** Explain why your answer is reasonable.

Practice Video Tools Games

Another Look!

A kindergarten teacher wants to buy individual boxes of crayons for her students. Each box contains 50 crayons. How many crayons will she have if she buys 30 boxes of crayons?

Use basic facts and place value to find 50×30.

$50 \times 30 = 5$ tens $\times 3$ tens
$= 15$ hundreds
$= 1,500$

So, $50 \times 30 = 1,500$.

The kindergarten teacher will have 1,500 crayons.

You can multiply with mental math by using basic facts and place-value strategies or you can break apart numbers and use properties of operations to solve.

Leveled Practice For **1–12**, use basic facts and place-value strategies to find each product.

1. $20 \times 20 =$ _____
     $=$ _____
     $=$ _____

2. $60 \times 30 =$ _____
     $=$ _____
     $=$ _____

3. $50 \times 60 =$ _____
     $=$ _____
     $=$ _____

4. 30×80

5. 60×60

6. 50×90

7. 30×70

8. 70×60

9. 40×50

10. 10×90

11. 40×10

12. 10×50

For **13–21**, find the missing factor.

13. $10 \times$ _____ $= 200$

14. $40 \times$ _____ $= 3,600$

15. $50 \times$ _____ $= 4,000$

16. $70 \times$ _____ $= 700$

17. $30 \times$ _____ $= 2,700$

18. _____ $\times 70 = 3,500$

19. _____ $\times 90 = 7,200$

20. $20 \times$ _____ $= 1,800$

21. $40 \times$ _____ $= 3,200$

22. Algebra Ms. Marks records the number of words each typist can type in 1 minute. How many more words could the fastest typist type in 30 minutes than the slowest typist? Use place-value strategies. Write and solve equations.

Typing Rates in 1 min	
Typist	**Words**
Lavon	50
Jerome	40
Charlie	60

23. Amy says, "To find 50 × 20, I multiply 5 × 2 and then place the total number of zeros in both factors at the end." Do you agree? Explain.

24. Algebra If in one year a city recorded a total of 97 rainy days, how many of the days did it **NOT** rain? Write and solve an equation.

365 days	
97	d

25. Name two 2-digit factors whose product is greater than 200 but less than 600.

26. Higher Order Thinking For every 30 minutes of television airtime, there are 8 minutes of commercials. If 90 minutes of television are aired, how many minutes of commercials will there be?

☑ Assessment Practice

27. The product of two factors is 7,200. If one of the factors is 90, what is the other factor?

Ⓐ 8,000   Ⓒ 80

Ⓑ 800   Ⓓ 8

28. Find 20 × 70.

Ⓐ 140   Ⓒ 1,000

Ⓑ 1,400   Ⓓ 2,000

Use basic facts to help find the missing factors.

Another Look!

You can use arrays, area models, or place-value blocks to help find the product of 20 × 14.

20 × 14 means 20 groups of 14, or (20 groups of 10) + (20 groups of 4).

Add the partial products from the model.

20 groups of 10 = 200
20 groups of 4 = 80

200 + 80 = 280

So, 20 × 14 = 280.

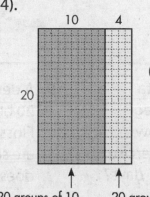

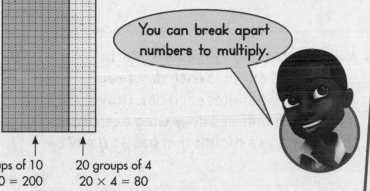

You can break apart numbers to multiply.

20 groups of 10
20 × 10 = 200

20 groups of 4
20 × 4 = 80

For 1–2, use the array to find each product.

1. 10 × 12

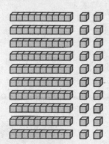

10 groups of 10 = _____

10 groups of 2 = _____

_____ + _____ = _____

So, 10 × 12 = _____.

2. 20 × 18

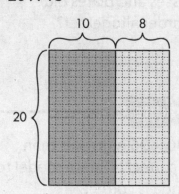

20 groups of 10 = _____

20 groups of 8 = _____

_____ + _____ = _____

So, 20 × 18 = _____.

For 3–6, find each product. Draw an array or an area model to help.

3. 50 × 15   **4.** 40 × 22   **5.** 30 × 39   **6.** 60 × 21

7. The height of each story of an apartment building is measured from the bottom of one floor to the bottom of the next floor. Each story has a height of 18 feet. How tall is the building?

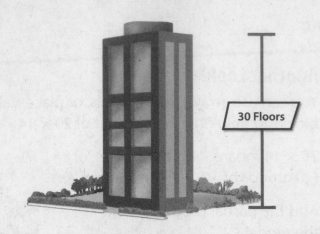

30 Floors

8. Make Sense and Persevere Marta exercises 30 minutes each day. Greg exercises 40 minutes each day. How many more minutes does Greg exercise than Marta in a month that has 31 days?

9. A dentist orders 15 boxes of floss and 20 boxes of toothbrushes each month. Floss is sold 70 to a box and toothbrushes are sold 50 to a box. How many items does the dentist order each month?

10. Mrs. Harrigan ordered 30 boxes of glasses for her restaurant. Each box holds 16 glasses. She also ordered 30 boxes of plates. There are 25 plates in each box. How many glasses and plates did Mrs. Harrigan order altogether?

11. Higher Order Thinking Without multiplying, is the product of 45×10 or 50×10 greater? Explain.

✓ **Assessment Practice**

12. Miranda says 30×26 is greater than 20×36. Is she correct? Draw a model to explain if Miranda is correct.

You can draw an area model or an array to represent the problem.

Practice Video Tools Games

Another Look!

A roller coaster has 38 seats for passengers. The roller coaster runs 24 times each hour. About how many passengers can ride the roller coaster each hour?

Choose numbers close to 38 and 24 that you can multiply mentally.

Step 1

Choose compatible numbers.

24 is close to 25.

38 is close to 40.

24×38

$\downarrow \quad \downarrow$

25×40

Step 2

Multiply the compatible numbers.

$25 \times 40 = 1,000$

So, 24×38 is about 1,000.

About 1,000 passengers can ride the roller coaster each hour.

For **1–16,** estimate each product.

1. 23×12

23 is close to 25.

12 is close to _____.

$25 \times$ _____ = _____

2. 24×31

24 is close to 25.

31 is close to _____.

_____ × _____ = _____

3. 19×24

4. 51×17

5. 82×78

6. 12×26

7. 24×62

8. 48×29

9. 53×39

10. 51×23

11. 53×54

12. 68×39

13. 29×43

14. 62×87

15. 36×42

16. 91×77

There is more than one way to estimate a product.

17. About how many gallons of water are used to refill the bathtub every day for 31 days? Explain.

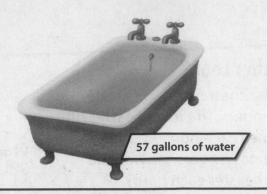

57 gallons of water

18. (A-Z) **Vocabulary** Use a vocabulary term to complete the definition.

_____ are numbers that are easy to compute mentally.

19. A store sells about 45 gadgets a day, 7 days a week. About how many gadgets might the store sell in 4 weeks? Explain.

20. Number Sense Nathan estimates 67×36 by finding 70×40. Will Nathan's estimate be greater than or less than the actual product? Explain.

21. Higher Order Thinking What might you consider when deciding whether to use rounding or compatible numbers to estimate? Explain.

☑ **Assessment Practice**

22. A tour guide leads groups of 26 people through a museum. She led 42 groups last year. Choose compatible numbers from the box to write two different estimates for the total number of people she led last year. Find the estimated products.

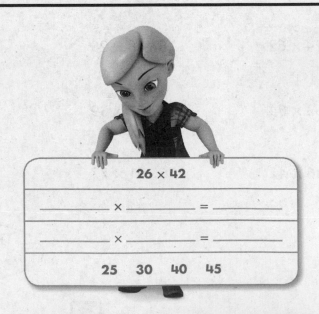

26×42

_____ × _____ = _____

_____ × _____ = _____

25   30   40   45

Name _____

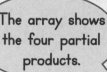

Another Look!

One way to find the product of 12 × 24 is to use an array.

Draw an array on a grid. Divide the array into tens and ones for each factor. Find the number of squares in each smaller rectangle. Then add the numbers of squares in the four smaller rectangles.

The array shows the four partial products.

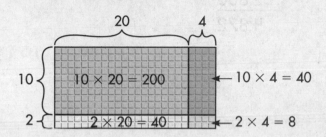

$$
\begin{array}{r}
8 \\
40 \\
40 \\
+\ 200 \\
\hline
288
\end{array}
$$

So, 12 × 24 = 288.

For **1–4**, find each product. Use the arrays drawn on grids to help.

1. 26 × 18

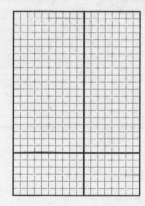

2. 23 × 23

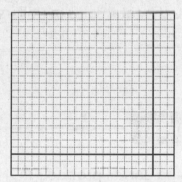

3. 19 × 27

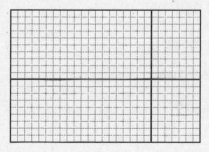

4. 11 × 16

5. Barb exercises for 22 hours each week. How many hours does she exercise in 14 weeks? Use the array drawn on the grid to help multiply.

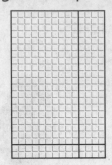

6. Teri used place value to find the product below. Is Teri's answer reasonable? Explain.

$$
\begin{array}{r}
4{,}296 \\
\times\ \ \ \ 7 \\
\hline
42 \\
630 \\
1{,}400 \\
2{,}800 \\
\underline{} \\
4{,}872
\end{array}
$$

7. Higher Order Thinking The prices at Nolan's Novelties store are shown at the right. If 27 boxes of neon keychains and 35 boxes of glow-in-the-dark pens were sold, what were the total sales in dollars?

Item	Price per Box
Neon keychains	$15
Glow-in-the-dark pens	$10

DATA

Assessment Practice

8. Insert the missing partial products in each equation. Then add to find the product.

300   240   42   1,200   140   20   16

$$
\begin{array}{r}
18 \\
\times 32 \\
\hline
16 \\
\square \\
240 \\
+\ \square
\end{array}
\qquad
\begin{array}{r}
47 \\
\times 26 \\
\hline
42 \\
\square \\
\square \\
+800
\end{array}
$$

9. Insert the missing factor in each equation.

39   53   78   51   37   26   23   83

$18 \times \square = 918$

$65 \times \square = 2{,}535$

$\square \times 27 = 2{,}106$

$23 \times \square = 529$

Name _____

Practice Video Tools Games

Another Look!

Find 23 × 18.

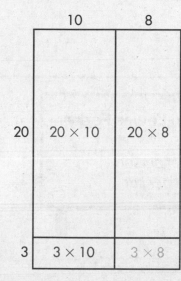

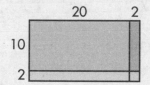
You can use an area model to show how you break apart the factors because there is more than one way. Then use the Distributive Property to help multiply.

$23 \times 18 = (20 + 3) \times (10 + 8)$

$= (20 + 3) \times 10 + (20 + 3) \times 8$

$= (20 \times 10) + (3 \times 10) + (20 \times 8) + (3 \times 8)$

$= 200 + 30 + 160 + 24$

$= 414$

For **1–3**, use the area model to find each product.

1. 14 × 19

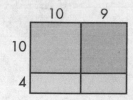

2. 12 × 22

3. 21 × 51

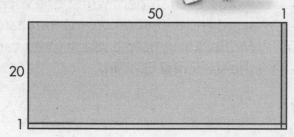

For **4–13**, draw an area model to find each product. Use properties of operations.

4. 10 ×18	**5.** 28 ×38	**6.** 51 ×12	**7.** 73 ×13	**8.** 99 ×11
9. 16 ×14	**10.** 17 ×38	**11.** 56 ×17	**12.** 11 ×13	**13.** 29 ×64

14. There are 27 students in Ms. Langley's class. Each student is assigned 15 different math problems. How many math problems are assigned to the whole class?

15. An arena hosts a concert on Friday and a rodeo on Saturday. If 12,211 people attend the concert and 9,217 attend the rodeo, how many people visit the arena on Friday and Saturday?

16. Number Sense On one trip, 82 people and 49 cars rode the ferry. About how much money did the ferry service collect for the one trip?

Cape May–Lewes Ferry

$3 per person
$34 per car

17. Higher Order Thinking Mr. Buckham teaches vocabulary to a class of 27 fourth-grade students. There are 63 new vocabulary words. Each student writes one vocabulary word and definition on an index card. Does Mr. Buckham have enough index cards for all the students? Explain.

Mr. Buckham has 1,500 index cards.

✓ **Assessment Practice**

18. Select all of the partial products which would be used to find 17 × 28.

☐ 200; 14; 8; 56
☐ 65; 80; 14; 2,000
☐ 56; 140; 80; 200
☐ 200; 140; 80; 56
☐ 2,000; 1,400; 80; 56

19. Select all of the ways you can use breaking apart and the Distributive Property to find the product of 45 × 18.

☐ 45 × (20 − 2)
☐ (40 × 10) + (5 × 8)
☐ (40 × 5) + (10 × 2)
☐ (40 × 10) + (40 × 8) + (5 × 10) + (5 × 8)
☐ (40 × 18) + (5 × 18)

Name _____

Additional Practice 4-6
Use Partial Products to Multiply by 2-Digit Numbers

Another Look!

Golf balls come in a box of 12. How many golf balls are in 14 boxes? Remember to estimate so you can tell if your answer is reasonable.

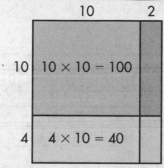

	10	2
10	$10 \times 10 = 100$	$10 \times 2 = 20$
4	$4 \times 10 = 40$	$4 \times 2 = 8$

$$\begin{array}{r} 12 \\ \times\ 14 \\ \hline 8 \\ 40 \\ 20 \\ +\ 100 \\ \hline 168 \end{array}$$

$4 \times 2 = 8$ ones
4×1 ten $= 4$ tens
10×2 ones $= 20$
10×1 ten $= 100$

There are 168 golf balls in the boxes.

For **1–8**, estimate. Find all the partial products. Then add to find the final product. Draw area models as needed.

1. $\begin{array}{r} 16 \\ \times\ 15 \\ \hline \end{array}$

2. $\begin{array}{r} 16 \\ \times\ 12 \\ \hline \end{array}$

3. $\begin{array}{r} 19 \\ \times\ 13 \\ \hline \end{array}$

4. $\begin{array}{r} 24 \\ \times\ 12 \\ \hline \end{array}$

5. $\begin{array}{r} 32 \\ \times\ 23 \\ \hline \end{array}$

6. $\begin{array}{r} 79 \\ \times\ 47 \\ \hline \end{array}$

7. $\begin{array}{r} 23 \\ \times\ 46 \\ \hline \end{array}$

8. $\begin{array}{r} 82 \\ \times\ 74 \\ \hline \end{array}$

9. Reasoning Why can the calculations to the right of each partial product be thought of as simpler problems?

```
      34
   ×  24
      16     4 × 4
     120     4 × 3 tens
      80     2 tens × 4
   + 600     2 tens × 3 tens
     816
```

10. Explain the mistakes in the calculation below. Show the correct calculation.

```
      12
   ×  13
       6
       3
      20
   +  10
      39
```

11. A movie theater charges $10 for an adult ticket and $9 for a child ticket. The goal is to make $1,200 on adult tickets each week. Did the theater make its goal this week? How much more or less than the goal did the theater make?

Weekday Movie Matinee Ticket Sales

12. Higher Order Thinking A golf practice range has 245 balls. The owner bought a carton of golf balls. How many golf balls does the owner have after buying the carton?

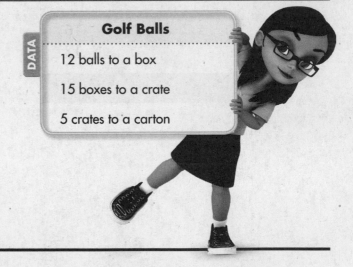

DATA

Golf Balls

12 balls to a box

15 boxes to a crate

5 crates to a carton

✓ **Assessment Practice**

13. Which set of numbers has the missing partial product and the final product?

```
      12
   ×  18
      16
      80
      20
   +  ☐
   ─────
     ☐
```

Ⓐ 100; 216

Ⓑ 10; 126

Ⓒ 106; 212

Ⓓ 100; 261

14. Select all the equations in which 15 is the missing factor.

☐ $b \times 15 = 225$

☐ $32 \times b = 480$

☐ $51 \times b = 765$

☐ $b \times 41 = 1,025$

☐ $65 \times b = 910$

Another Look!

April needs to arrange 18 baskets with each containing 15 silk plants. She needs 8 silk flowers on each plant. How many silk flowers will be in all the baskets?

Tell how you can make sense of the problem to solve.

- I can identify the quantities given.

- I can understand how the quantities are related.

- I can choose and implement an appropriate strategy.

When you make sense and persevere, you use objects or diagrams to make sense of problems.

Find how many silk plants April needs.

$p = 15$ plants $\times$ 18 baskets

$15 \times 18 = 15 \times (20 - 2)$

$\qquad = (15 \times 20) - (15 \times 2)$

$\qquad = 300 - 30$

$\qquad = 270$

April needs 270 silk plants.

Then, find how many silk flowers will be in all the baskets.

$f = 270$ plants $\times$ 8 flowers

$8 \times 270 = 8 \times (200 + 70)$

$\qquad = (8 \times 200) + (8 \times 70)$

$\qquad = 1,600 + 560$

$\qquad = 2,160$

There will be 2,160 flowers in all the baskets.

Make Sense and Persevere

A store received a shipment of 4 boxes of peanuts. All four boxes were stacked on top of each other and measured 12 feet high. How many ounces of peanuts did the store receive? Use Exercises 1–4 to answer the question.

PEANUTS

Contents: 24 bags

12 oz in each bag

1. What do you know and what do you need to find?

2. What steps might you take to solve the problem?

3. Do you think the store got more or less than 800 ounces of peanuts? Justify your answer.

4. How many ounces of peanuts did the store receive? Explain.

Cameras

A purchasing manager for an electronics store has a choice between two digital cameras. Information about each camera is shown below. How much money can the store make with Camera 1? The money the store makes is the difference in the price of what the store sells the camera for and the price of what the store pays to buy the camera.

Camera 1
Store price: $46
Selling price: $85
Store can buy: 21

Camera 2
Store price: $62
Selling price: $98
Store can buy: 16

5. Make Sense and Persevere What are the hidden questions that must be answered before finding the solution to the problem?

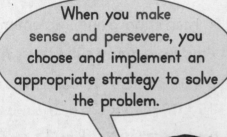

When you make sense and persevere, you choose and implement an appropriate strategy to solve the problem.

6. Model with Math How can you use objects, pictures, or diagrams and equations to represent and solve this problem?

7. Look for Relationships How can you tell that your answer makes sense? Explain.

Additional Practice 5-2
Mental Math: Estimate Quotients

Another Look!

Estimate $460 \div 9$.

Here are two ways to estimate quotients.

One Way

Use compatible numbers.

What number close to 460 can be easily divided by 9? Try 450.

$450 \div 9 = 50$

$460 \div 9$ is about 50.

Another Way

Use multiplication.

Nine times what number is about 460?

$9 \times 5 = 45$, so $9 \times 50 = 450$.

$460 \div 9$ is about 50.

For **1–20**, estimate each quotient. Show your work.

1. $165 \div 4$ **2.** $35 \div 4$ **3.** $715 \div 9$ **4.** $490 \div 8$

5. $512 \div 5$ **6.** $652 \div 8$ **7.** $790 \div 9$ **8.** $200 \div 7$

9. $311 \div 6$ **10.** $162 \div 2$ **11.** $418 \div 6$ **12.** $554 \div 7$

13. $92 \div 3$ **14.** $351 \div 7$ **15.** $497 \div 5$ **16.** $61 \div 2$

17. $202 \div 2$ **18.** $153 \div 3$ **19.** $98 \div 9$ **20.** $174 \div 9$

For **21–23**, use Franny's To-Do List.

21. Franny has 5 pages left in the album. About how many pictures can she place on each remaining page?

22. Franny plans to spend 4 hours reading. About how many pages would she need to read each hour to finish the book?

23. Franny wants to spend an equal amount of money on the presents for her friends. If she has $62, about how much money can she spend on each present?

Franny's To-Do List
• Put 64 pictures in a photo album.
• Finish reading 113 pages of a book.
• Buy presents for Kate, Wendy, and Tia.
• Put shoes on rack.

24. **Model with Math** The veterinarian has seen 47 dogs, 19 cats, 7 exotic birds, and 3 horses this week. Complete the bar diagram and find the total number of animals seen by the veterinarian this week.

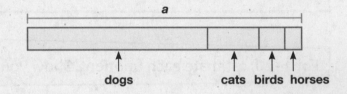

dogs   cats birds horses

25. Wayne has 303 marbles. If he gives away 123 of the marbles equally to 3 friends, about how many marbles will Wayne give each friend? How many marbles does Wayne have left?

26. **Higher Order Thinking** Tessa wants to separate 187 ears of corn into bags of 6 ears each. She has 35 bags. Estimate to find whether Tessa has enough bags. Explain.

✅ **Assessment Practice**

27. Deon set a goal to ride his bicycle 310 miles in a month. He has biked 145 miles so far. If there are 4 days left in the month, about how many miles should Deon ride each day to reach his goal? Explain.

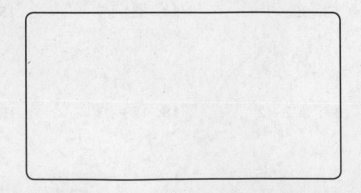

Name _____

Another Look!

A honeybee can travel 2,925 feet in 3 minutes. How many feet would that be each minute?

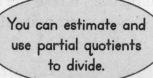

$$
\begin{array}{r}
5 \\
70 \\
900
\end{array}\Big\} 975
$$

$$
\begin{array}{r}
3\overline{)2,925} \\
-\,2,700 \\
\hline
225 \\
-\,210 \\
\hline
15 \\
-\,15 \\
\hline
0
\end{array}
$$

You can estimate and use partial quotients to divide.

The honeybee can travel 975 feet each minute.

For **1–16**, use partial quotients to divide.

1. $9\overline{)126}$ **2.** $7\overline{)474}$ **3.** $2\overline{)179}$ **4.** $6\overline{)237}$

5. $4\overline{)3,264}$ **6.** $8\overline{)3,349}$ **7.** $3\overline{)6,334}$ **8.** $5\overline{)8,248}$

9. $6\overline{)5,769}$ **10.** $3\overline{)441}$ **11.** $7\overline{)4,999}$ **12.** $6\overline{)4,272}$

13. $3\overline{)3,791}$ **14.** $9\overline{)756}$ **15.** $5\overline{)4,271}$ **16.** $4\overline{)1,847}$

17. **Algebra** Abigail is planning a 90-meter sack-relay race for field day. Each team member will hop 6 meters. How many members, *m*, does Abigail need on each team? Write and solve an equation.

18. **enVision® STEM** The function of a hydroelectric plant is to change the energy from the motion of water into electricity. How long does it take the hydroelectric plant shown to produce 384-kilowatt hours of electricity?

A hydroelectric plant can produce 8 kilowatt hours of electricity each hour.

19. **Critique Reasoning** Tell whether Miranda's or Jesse's reasoning is correct. Explain.

Miranda
$$6{,}050 \div 5 = (6{,}000 + 50) \div 5$$
$$= (6{,}000 \div 5) + (50 \div 5)$$
$$= 1{,}200 + 10$$
$$= 1{,}210$$

Jesse
$$6{,}050 \div 5 = (6{,}000 + 50) \div (3+2)$$
$$= (6{,}000 \div 3) + (50 \div 2)$$
$$= 2{,}000 + 25$$
$$= 2{,}025$$

20. Kelli signed up for 38 gymnastics lessons. Each lesson lasts for 2 hours. How many hours of lessons did Kelli sign up for?

21. **Higher Order Thinking** How could you use the Distributive Property to find $1{,}484 \div 7$?

22. Select all correct combinations of partial quotients and a remainder which can be used to find $4{,}306 \div 9$.

☐ 300, 100, 60, 2, R8

☐ 300, 100, 70, 8 R4

☐ 400, 60, 10, 8 R4

☐ 400, 60, 2 R 8

☐ 400, 70, 8, R4

Name _____

Another Look!
Find 78 ÷ 5.

You can draw pictures to help solve division problems.

First, divide the tens.

There is 1 ten in each of the 5 groups.

78 ÷ 5 = 15 R3

Then, unbundle the 2 tens for 20 ones.

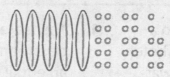

20 ones and 8 ones are equal to 28 ones.

Finally, divide the ones.

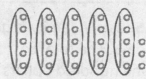

Each of the 5 groups has 1 ten and 5 ones. There are 3 ones remaining.

For **1–8**, Use place-value blocks or a drawing to divide. Record remainders.

1. 66 ÷ _____ = _____ R2

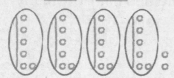

2. 136 ÷ 4 = _____

3. 131 ÷ _____ = _____ R1

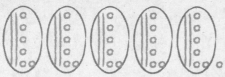

4. 76 ÷ _____ = _____ R _____

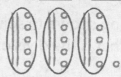

5. 140 ÷ 6

6. 95 ÷ 2

7. 96 ÷ 8

8. 51 ÷ 2

9. Marcos has 78 toy cars. He arranges the toy cars into 6 equal groups. How many toy cars are in each group? Complete the diagram started below to show your work.

Pictures can help you solve problems.

10. **Number Sense** A family is going on a trip for 3 days. The total cost for the hotel is $336. One hundred dollars a day was budgeted for food. How much will each day of the trip cost?

11. There are 37 chairs and 9 tables in a classroom. Mrs. Kensington wants to put an equal number of chairs at each table. How many chairs can she put at each table? Will there be any chairs left over?

12. **Higher Order Thinking** Mrs. Dryson divided her collection of 52 glass bears into equal groups. She had 1 bear left over. How many groups did Mrs. Dryson make? How many bears are in each group?

13. Ben has 165 pictures from his summer trip to Austria. He put 6 pictures on each page of a photo album. How many pages of the album did Ben fill? How many pages did Ben use?

14. Adrian used the drawing shown to solve a division sentence. What is the division sentence? Explain.

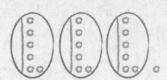

15. What is $59 \div 4$?

   Ⓐ 5 R4

   Ⓑ 6 R1

   Ⓒ 14 R3

   Ⓓ 7 R2

16. What is the missing divisor?
   $966 \div n = 161$

   Ⓐ 5

   Ⓑ 6

   Ⓒ 7

   Ⓓ 8

Practice Video Tools Games

Another Look!

Molly is making tissue-paper flowers. She has 240 sheets of pink tissue paper and 260 sheets of yellow tissue paper. How many flowers will Molly be able to make with all her tissue paper?

> 7 sheets of any color tissue paper to make each flower

How can you model with math?

- I can use pictures, objects, and equations to show how to solve this problem.

- I can improve my math model if needed.

Find the hidden question and use equations to answer it.

How much tissue paper does Molly have in all?

t, tissue paper

240	260

$240 + 260 = t$
$t = 500$
Molly has 500 sheets of tissue paper.

Use equations and the answer to the hidden question to answer the original question.

How many flowers, *f*, will Molly be able to make?

$f = 500 \div 7$.
$f = 71 \text{ R}3$

Molly can make 71 tissue-paper flowers.

Model with Math

A school baseball team raised $810 for new uniforms. Each player on the team sold one book of tickets. There were 10 tickets in a book and each ticket cost $3. How many tickets were sold?

1. What equation can you write and solve to find the cost, *b*, of each book of tickets sold?

2. Write and solve an equation to find the number of tickets, *t*, sold. Explain.

3. Write and solve an equation to find the number of players, *p*, on the baseball team.

Yoga

Yoga classes are offered 2 days a week for 6 weeks at both the community center and the local gym. The cost for the classes at the community center is $72, plus an additional one-time fee of $12 to rent the yoga equipment used in class. The cost at the local gym is $8 a class. Regina wants to know which class she can take for less money.

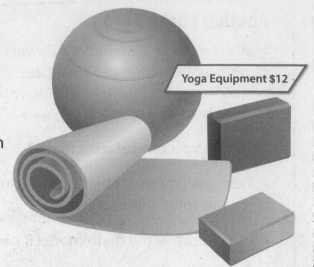

Yoga Equipment $12

4. **Reasoning** What are the quantities given in the problem, and how are they related?

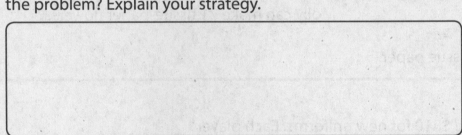

5. **Make Sense and Persevere** What is a good plan for solving the problem? Explain your strategy.

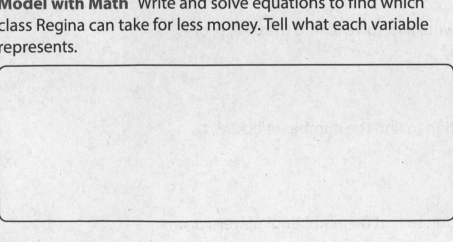

When you model with math, you use equations to model the problem.

6. **Model with Math** Write and solve equations to find which class Regina can take for less money. Tell what each variable represents.

Another Look!

Darrell has 3 cousins. Robert has 42 cousins. How many times as many cousins does Robert have as Darrell?

Let n = the number of times as many.

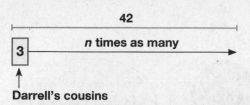

Darrell's cousins

Write a multiplication equation to compare the numbers of cousins.

42 is n times as many as 3.

$42 = n \times 3$

What number times 3 equals 42?

> Since you know the original amount and the total, you need to divide to find how many times as many.

Write and solve a related division equation.

If $42 = n \times 3$, then $n = 42 \div 3$.

$n = 14$

Robert has 14 times as many cousins as Darrell.

$$
\begin{array}{r}
4 \\
10 \\
3\overline{)42} \\
-30 \\
\hline
12 \\
-12 \\
\hline
0
\end{array} \Big\} 14
$$

For **1–4**, write a comparison sentence and an equation. Find the value of the variable that makes the sentence true.

1. There are 51 families in Oakville who have a pool. That is 3 times as many families with a pool than in Elmburg. How many families in Elmburg, n, have a pool?

2. Gilbert walked 288 minutes. That is 4 times as many minutes as Eileen walked. How many minutes, m, did Eileen walk?

3. Marcy picked 3 times as many ounces of kale as Phil picked. Phil picked 42 ounces of kale. How many ounces of kale, k, did Marcy pick?

4. Jennifer feeds 5 times as many fish as Tony. Tony feeds 56 fish. How many fish, f, does Jennifer feed?

5. **Algebra** The yellow T-shirt costs how many times as much as the blue T-shirt? Draw a bar diagram and write and solve an equation.

6. **Algebra** Mason is 9 years old. His mother's age is 4 times Mason's age. How old is Mason's mother? Draw a bar diagram and write and solve an equation.

You can multiply to find Mason's mother's age.

7. **Reasoning** Hilary walked 654 feet in 3 minutes. She says she walked 218 feet per minute. Is Hilary's answer reasonable? Explain.

8. **Higher Order Thinking** The value of n is both 5 times as much as the value of m and 36 more than the value of m. What are the values of n and m? Explain.

☑ **Assessment Practice**

9. Debbie has 8 quarters and 24 pennies in her piggy bank. She has n times as many pennies as quarters. Which equation can be used to find n?

Ⓐ $n = 8 \times 24$

Ⓑ $24 = 4 + n$

Ⓒ $24 = n \div 8$

Ⓓ $24 = n \times 8$

10. Marcus sleeps 60 hours a week. This is 5 times as many hours as he plays chess. How many hours a week does Marcus play chess?

Ⓐ 11 hours

Ⓑ 12 hours

Ⓒ 13 hours

Ⓓ 14 hours

Practice Video Tools Games

Another Look!

There are 150 students in band. The boys and girls are in separate rows. There are 6 students in each row. There are 12 rows of boys. How many rows of girls are there?

Step 1

Write an expression to represent the number of boys in band.

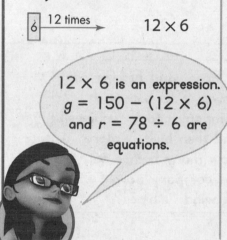

6 — 12 times → 12 × 6

12 × 6 is an expression. $g = 150 - (12 × 6)$ and $r = 78 ÷ 6$ are equations.

Step 2

Write and solve an equation to find the number of girls in band.

g = the number of girls

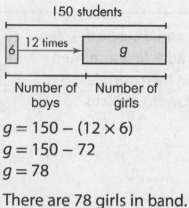

150 students

6 — 12 times → g

Number of boys   Number of girls

$g = 150 - (12 × 6)$
$g = 150 - 72$
$g = 78$

There are 78 girls in band.

Step 3

Write and solve an equation to find the rows of girls in band.

r = the number of rows of girls

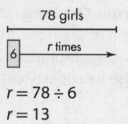

78 girls

6 — r times →

$r = 78 ÷ 6$
$r = 13$

There are 13 rows of girls.

For **1–2**, draw bar diagrams and write equations to solve each problem. Use variables to represent unknown quantities and tell what each variable represents.

1. Friday night, a pizza parlor sold 5 large pizzas and some medium pizzas. The pizza parlor made a total of $291. How many medium pizzas were sold?

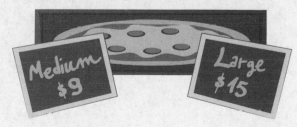

Medium $9   Large $15

2. What is the area of the giant American flag shown?

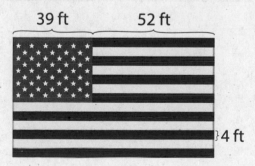

39 ft   52 ft

34 ft

3. Emma has $100 to spend at the pet store. She needs to buy 1 bag of dog food and 2 chew toys. How many catnip toys can Emma buy? Write equations to show each step.

Barky's Pet Store

Product	Cost
Bag of Dog Food	$35
Bag of Cat Food	$18
Chew Toy	$12
Catnip Toy	$9

4. **Higher Order Thinking** Maurice and Trina both solve the problem at the right. Maurice adds first and then multiplies. Trina multiplies first and then adds. Who is correct? Use a property of operations to explain.

> A large wind turbine can power 598 homes. A company had 4 turbines and then built 5 more. How many homes can the company power with its wind turbines?

☑ **Assessment Practice**

5. A science teacher has $225 to spend on lab equipment. He buys 4 posters with a guide to classifying rocks, for $19 each. Student rock collections cost $9 each. How many rock collections can he buy? Explain how you solve. Use one or more equations and bar diagrams in your explanation. Tell what your variables represent.

Name _____

Another Look!

Bella bakes 3 batches of homemade dog treats one day and 4 batches the next. Each batch has 24 treats. She sells bags with 6 treats in each. How many bags can she fill?

You usually can solve multi-step problems in more than one way.

One Way

t = the number of treats Bella made
$t = (3 + 4) \times 24$
$t = 168$

b = the number of bags Bella can fill
$b = 168 \div 6$
$b = 28$

Bella can fill 28 bags.

Another Way

b = the number of bags Bella can fill from each batch
$b = 24 \div 6$
$b = 4$

t = the total number of bags Bella can fill
$t = (3 + 4) \times 4$
$t = 28$

Bella can fill 28 bags

For **1–2**, draw bar diagrams, and write equations to solve each problem. Use variables to represent unknown quantities and tell what each variable represents.

1. Four people at Pia's Pottery Shop each make 29 mugs and 18 pottery bowls. Three people at Jason's Craft Shop each make the same number of mugs and twice as many bowls. How many objects did the seven people make in all?

2. The third-grade class collected 148 books to donate to the library. The fourth-grade class collected 175 books. The students need to pack the books into boxes. Each box holds 9 books. How many boxes do they need to hold all the books?

3. Brendan, Zach, and their father have $30 to spend at the county fair. Brendan and Zach qualify for a child's price. How many times can all 3 go on the boat rides? Draw bar diagrams and write one or more equations to show how you solve. Tell what your variables represent.

County Fair		
Kind of Ticket	Adult	Child
Admission	$8	$4
Boat Rides	$2	$1

DATA

4. **Higher Order Thinking** Izzy and Ela both solve the problem below correctly. Explain how each solve.

How much does it cost for 2 adults and 4 children to go to the fair and take a boat ride?

Izzy

$8 + 2 = 10$
$4 + 1 = 5$
$C = cost$
$C = (2 \times 10) + (4 \times 5)$

$C = \$40$

It costs $40.

Ela

$A = cost\ for\ admission$
$A = (2 \times 8) + (4 \times 4)$
$A = \$32$
$B = cost\ for\ boat\ ride$
$B = (2 \times 2) + (4 \times 1)$
$B = \$8$
$T = the\ total\ cost$
$T = 32 + 8 = \$40$

she found the total cost. Ela found the total cost for admission

Assessment Practice

5. Kate's dad gives each of his 5 children an equal part of $340 to buy gifts. Kate adds $28 to her portion. She finds classic DVDs for $8 each. How many DVDs can Kate buy? Explain how you solve. Use one or more equations and bar diagrams in your explanation. Tell what your variables represent.

Another Look!

A museum director would like to display butterflies and dragonflies in 5 cases with about the same number of insects in each case. How many insects should go in each case?

Identify the hidden questions.

- How many butterflies are there?

- How many insects are there?

Write and solve equations to solve the hidden questions and the main question.

Let b = the number of butterflies.

$b = 3 \times 36$, $b = 108$ butterflies.

Let i = the number of insects.

$i = 36 + 108$, $i = 144$ insects

Let c = the number of cases.

$c = 144 \div 5$, $c = 28$ R4

28 insects should go in one display case and 29 insects should go in each of the other 4 cases.

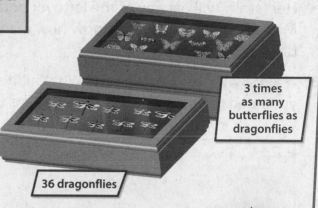

3 times as many butterflies as dragonflies

36 dragonflies

You can make sense of problems by finding the hidden questions.

Make Sense and Persevere

The diagram shows how many laps three friends swim each week. How can you determine the number of miles Ariel swam?

1. Write the hidden question(s) you need to answer before you answer the original question. Use equations to solve.

MacKenzie: 28 laps

June: 3 times as many laps as MacKenzie

Ariel: 20 more laps than June

8 laps equal a mile

2. Use your answers to the hidden question(s) and an equation to determine how many miles, m, Ariel swam.

Selling Potatoes

Ms. Sacksteader owns a grocery store. She buys 272 pounds of potatoes for $99. She wants to sell them for twice as much. She makes 9 bags containing 10 pounds each and puts the rest in 5-pound bags. Her family will eat any of the leftover potatoes. Ms. Sacksteader wants to know how many 5-pound bags of potatoes she can sell.

3. Make Sense and Persevere What hidden questions do you need to answer first? Use equations to solve each.

Each 5-pound bag of potatoes sells for $4.

Be sure to tell what each variable represents.

4. Model with Math How many 5-pound bags of potatoes can Ms. Sacksteader sell? Use equations to solve. Explain your answer.

5. Be Precise How much money will Ms. Sacksteader make for the 5-pound bags? Write and solve an equation to show how to solve.

Name _____

Additional Practice 7-1
Understand Factors

Another Look!

Mark is rearranging 15 desks in his classroom. Use the grid to show all the ways the desks could be arranged in a rectangular array. What are the factor pairs of 15?

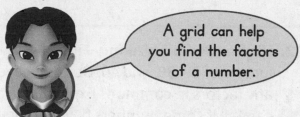

A grid can help you find the factors of a number.

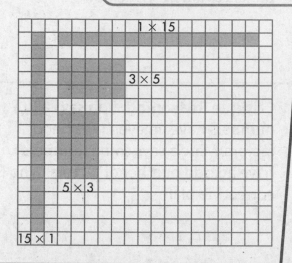

Mark can arrange the desks in 4 different ways.

The factor pairs of 15 are 1 × 15 and 3 × 5.

For **1–2**, find all the possible arrays for each number. Use the arrays to help write the factor pairs.

1. 13

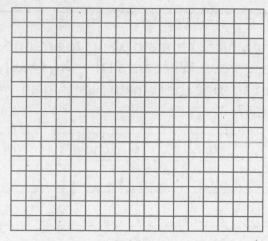

2. 10

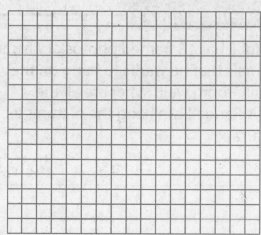

For **3–8**, use grids to find the factor pairs for each number.

3. 17

4. 37

5. 42

6. 29

7. 33

8. 48

9. enVision® STEM Solar panels use the sun's energy to generate power. A town wants to install 28 solar panels in an array. What are all the possible ways the panels could be installed?

10. Use grids to draw all the possible arrays for 5, 7, and 11. What do you notice about the arrays for these numbers?

11. Critique Reasoning Rob says all numbers have an even number of factors. Marcia says some numbers have an odd number of factors. Who is correct? Explain.

12. Higher Order Thinking Find all the factors of 38, 39, and 40. Do they have any factors in common? Explain how you can tell if some numbers have factors in common without finding the factors.

✓ **Assessment Practice**

13. Randall has 18 framed photos of African animals that he wants to hang on the family-room wall. What are all the ways Randall can hang the pictures in an array?

Rows	Pictures in Each Row

14. Molly has 20 tomato plants to arrange in her garden. What are all the ways Molly can arrange the tomato plants in an array?

Rows	plants in Each Row

Name _____

Additional Practice 7-2
Factors

Another Look!

Find the factors and factor pairs for 8.

1 group of 8   or 8 groups of 1

1×8

8×1

2 groups of 4   or 4 groups of 2

2×4

4×2

The factor pairs are 1 and 8, 2 and 4.
The factors of 8 are 1, 2, 4, and 8.

> When multiplying two numbers, both numbers are factors of the product.

For **1–6**, write the factor pairs for each number.

1. 75
1 and _____
_____ and 25
_____ and 15

2. 28
_____ and 28
_____ and 14
4 and _____

3. 46
_____ and 46
_____ and 23

4. 47

5. 77

6. 23

For **7–15**, write the factors of each number. Use counters to help as needed.

7. 74

8. 58

9. 44

10. 72

11. 57

12. 10

13. 7

14. 60

15. 66

16. Mr. Matthews purchases 22 boxes of pencils for 5 fourth-grade classes. Each box contains 45 pencils. How many pencils will each class receive?

17. Damita wants to read a 257-page book in one week. She plans to read 36 pages each day. Will she reach her goal? Explain.

18. Algebra Crystal has 81 buttons arranged equally in 3 rows. Write and solve an equation to find the number of buttons in each row.

19. Sal has 13 stamps arranged in an array. Describe Sal's array.

20. As part of her science project, Shay is making a model of a wind farm. She wants to put 24 turbines in her model. What arrays can Shay make using 24 turbines?

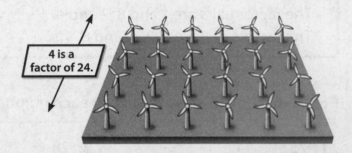

4 is a factor of 24.

21. Mrs. Fisher has 91 watches on display at her store. She says she can arrange them into rows and columns without any watches left over. Mr. Fisher says she can only make 1 row with all 91 watches. Who is correct? Explain.

22. Higher Order Thinking Mr. Deets is making an array to display 9 pictures. For each pair of different factors, there are two arrays he can make. How many different arrays can Mr. Deets make? Is the number of arrays odd or even? Explain.

23. Which number is not a factor of both 36 and 84?

Ⓐ 2

Ⓑ 3

Ⓒ 5

Ⓓ 6

24. Dana has some coins. She wants to display them in an array. Which of the following numbers of coins provides only 2 arrays for Dana to choose from?

Ⓐ 10

Ⓑ 16

Ⓒ 25

Ⓓ 29

Name _____

Another Look!

Silvia has 45 cans of paint to put on shelves. Each shelf can hold up to 15 cans of paint. Each row must have the same number of cans on the shelf. How many different ways might Silvia put the cans on the shelves?

Tell how you can generalize to find how many different ways Silvia can put the cans of paint on the shelves.

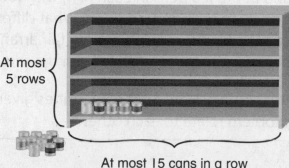

At most 5 rows

At most 15 cans in a row

- I can look for things that repeat in a problem.

- I can look for shortcuts.

- I can generalize from an example.

Find the factors of 45.

When you generalize, you look for steps that repeat.

1 × 45 = 45 and **45 × 1 = 45**
3 × 15 = 45 and **15 × 3 = 45**
5 × 9 = 45 and **9 × 5 = 45**
2, 4, 6, 7, and **8** are not factors.

The factors of **45** are **1, 3, 5, 9, 15,** and **45**.

Silvia can put the cans of paint on 5 shelves with 9 cans on each shelf or 3 shelves with 15 cans on each shelf.

Generalize

An auditorium has rows of seats with 8 seats in each row. Kayla knows there are at least 70 seats but fewer than 150 seats in the auditorium. How many rows of seats can there be in the auditorium? Use Exercises 1–3 to answer the question.

1. Explain how you would find the least possible number of rows in the auditorium.

2. How would you find all the possible numbers of rows, without having to check if 8 is a factor of every number between 70 and 150?

3. Name all the possible numbers of rows in the auditorium.

County Fair
At the county fair, animals are judged for the quality of their breeding and health. The animal pens are arranged in an array, with one animal in each pen. A barn can hold at most 10 rows of pens and at most 6 pens in each row, with room for people to walk around them. What different ways can the planners of the county fair arrange the pens for the horses and cows in the same barn?

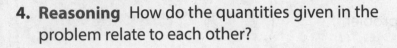 18 horses

22 cows

57 chickens

4. **Reasoning** How do the quantities given in the problem relate to each other?

5. **Make Sense and Persevere** What steps do you need to do first? Explain.

When you generalize, you find an efficient method for solving a problem, which can be used to solve similar problems.

6. **Model with Math** What are all the factor pairs for the sum of the horses and cows? Represent the factors with a diagram to show how you found all the factor pairs.

7. **Be Precise** What are all the different ways the planners can arrange the pens for the horses and cows in the barn?

Practice   Video   Tools   Games

Additional Practice 7-4
Prime and Composite Numbers

Another Look!

> You can look for factors to help you tell whether a number is prime or composite.

Is 15 a prime or a composite number? Find all the factors of 15.

Factors of 15: 1, 3, 5, 15

15 is a composite number because it has more than two factors.

Is 29 a prime or a composite number? Find all the factors of 29.

Factors of 29: 1, 29

29 is a prime number because it only has two factors, 1 and the number itself.

For **1–4**, use or draw arrays to tell whether each number is prime or composite.

1. 7

2. 9

3. 8

4. 4

For **5–16**, tell whether each number is prime or composite.

5. 81   **6.** 43   **7.** 72   **8.** 93

9. 53   **10.** 87   **11.** 13   **12.** 27

13. 88   **14.** 19   **15.** 69   **16.** 79

17. Use Structure Create a list of prime numbers from 1 to 100.

- Write all the numbers from 1 to 100.
- Draw a triangle around 1; it is neither prime nor composite.
- Circle 2 and cross out all other multiples of 2.
- Circle 3 and cross out all other multiples of 3.
- Circle 5 and cross out all other multiples of 5.
- Continue in the same way. The circled numbers are prime.

How many prime numbers are between 1 and 100?

△1	②	③	4̸	⑤
6̸	⑦	8̸	9̸	1̸0̸
⑪	1̸2̸	⑬	1̸4̸	1̸5̸
1̸6̸	⑰	1̸8̸	⑲	2̸0̸
2̸1̸	2̸2̸	㉓	2̸4̸	2̸5̸
2̸6̸	2̸7̸	2̸8̸	㉙	3̸0̸
㉛	3̸2̸	3̸3̸	3̸4̸	3̸5̸
3̸6̸	㊲	3̸8̸	3̸9̸	4̸0̸

18. Number Sense Are all odd numbers prime numbers? Explain.

19. Some plants have thorns for protection. Ben is a florist and cuts thorns from flowers. On Monday, he cut 267 thorns. On Tuesday, he cut 381 thorns. On Wednesday, he cut 522 thorns. How many thorns did Ben cut?

20. **Vocabulary** Use *prime* and *composite* to complete the definitions.

A _____ number is a whole number greater than 1 that has more than 2 factors. A _____ number is a whole number greater than 1 that has exactly two factors, 1 and itself.

21. Higher Order Thinking Larry says all numbers that have a 2 in the ones place are composite numbers. Explain if Larry is correct or incorrect.

☑ Assessment Practice

22. Which of the following digits might composite numbers greater than 10 have in the ones place? Select all that apply.

- ☐ 1
- ☐ 2
- ☐ 3
- ☐ 4
- ☐ 5

23. Which of the following digits might prime numbers greater than 10 have in the ones place? Select all that apply.

- ☐ 0
- ☐ 2
- ☐ 3
- ☐ 7
- ☐ 9

Name _____

Another Look!

What are some multiples of 7?

Step 1 Find the column (or row) for 7.

Step 2 All the numbers in that column (or row) are multiples of 7.

In the chart, the multiples of 7 are 7, 14, 21, 28, 35, 42, 49, 56, and 63.

7, 14, 21, 28, 35, 42, 49, 56, and 63 are multiples of 7 because $1 \times 7 = 7$, $2 \times 7 = 14$, $3 \times 7 = 21$, and so on.

You can use a multiplication chart to find multiples.

×	1	2	3	4	5	6	7	8	9
1	1	2	3	4	5	6	7	8	9
2	2	4	6	8	10	12	14	16	18
3	3	6	9	12	15	18	21	24	27
4	4	8	12	16	20	24	28	32	36
5	5	10	15	20	25	30	35	40	45
6	6	12	18	24	30	36	42	48	54
7	7	14	21	28	35	42	49	56	63
8	8	16	24	32	40	48	56	64	72
9	9	18	27	36	45	54	63	72	81

For **1–8**, write five multiples of each number.

1. 12

2. 18

3. 40

4. 16

5. 100

6. 25

7. 50

8. 63

For **9–20**, tell whether the first number is a multiple of the second number.

9. 21, 7

10. 28, 3

11. 17, 3

12. 20, 4

13. 55, 5

14. 15, 5

15. 26, 4

16. 32, 8

17. 48, 7

18. 60, 2

19. 79, 4

20. 81, 3

21. Is 6 a multiple or a factor of 12?

22. Is 8 a multiple or a factor of 4?

23. What number has factors of 2 and 3 and 12 and 18 as multiples?

24. What numbers have 12, 24, and 36 as multiples?

Make a list of the numbers that can be divided evenly by 2 and 3.

Make a list of the numbers that divide evenly into 12, 24, and 36.

For **25** and **26**, use the table at the right.

25. Paulo's family arrived at the reunion at 8:30 A.M. How long do they have before the trip to Scenic Lake Park?

26. How much longer is dinner than the slide show?

DATA	Suarez Family Reunion Schedule	
	Trip to Scenic Lake Park	10:15 A.M. to 2:30 P.M.
	Slide show	4:15 P.M. to 5:10 P.M.
	Dinner	5:30 P.M. to 7:00 P.M.
	Campfire	7:55 P.M. to 9:30 P.M.

27. Carmen listed the multiples of 24 as 1, 2, 3, 4, 6, 8, 12, and 24. Is she correct? Explain why or why not.

28. Higher Order Thinking What is the least multiple 6 and 8 have in common? Explain.

✓ **Assessment Practice**

29. Which numbers are **NOT** multiples of 6? Write all the numbers that are **NOT** multiples of 6.

1	2	6
18	26	36

NOT Multiples of 6

☐

☐

☐

30. Which multiples do 3 and 5 have in common? Write all the common multiples of 3 and 5.

3	5	15
30	33	35

Common Multiples of 3 and 5

☐

☐

Another Look!

Use an area model to find two fractions equivalent to $\frac{1}{2}$.

Many fractions are equivalent to $\frac{1}{2}$.

The circle is divided into 2 equal parts. The shaded part represents $\frac{1}{2}$.

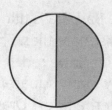

Divide the circle into 4 equal parts. The shaded part represents $\frac{2}{4}$.

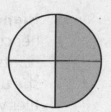

Divide the circle into 8 equal parts. The shaded part represents $\frac{4}{8}$.

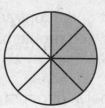

$\frac{1}{2}$, $\frac{2}{4}$, and $\frac{4}{8}$ are equivalent fractions.

1. Write a fraction equivalent to $\frac{3}{5}$.

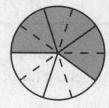

2. Write two fractions equivalent to $\frac{9}{12}$.

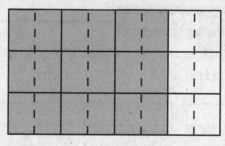

For **3–10**, draw an area model or use fraction strips to solve each problem.

3. $\frac{3}{5} = \frac{\square}{10}$

4. $\frac{3}{6} = \frac{\square}{12}$

5. $\frac{4}{10} = \frac{\square}{5}$

6. $\frac{3}{4} = \frac{\square}{8}$

7. $\frac{5}{10} = \frac{1}{\square}$

8. $\frac{4}{6} = \frac{\square}{12}$

9. $\frac{5}{5} = \frac{\square}{10}$

10. $\frac{1}{2} = \frac{6}{\square}$

11. Write two equivalent fractions to describe the portion of the eggs that are dark gray.

For **12–13**, use the table at the right.

12. The results of an election for mayor are shown at the right. Which candidate received the most votes and which received the least votes?

Candidate	Number of Votes
Leonard Hansen	12,409
Margaret O'Connor	12,926
Jillian Garcia	12,904

DATA

13. How many people voted for the three candidates?

14. Tell what operations are needed to solve the following problem. Then solve the problem.

The school auditorium has 22 rows with 28 seats each. At a school concert, 19 seats were empty. How many seats were filled?

15. Higher Order Thinking Barbara is tiling her craft room floor with square tiles. She wants $\frac{6}{10}$ of the square tiles to be red. If she uses 18 red tiles, how many square tiles will be used to cover the floor? Draw an area model to help solve.

✓ **Assessment Practice**

16. Select all the fractions that are equivalent to $\frac{3}{4}$. Use the area models to help.

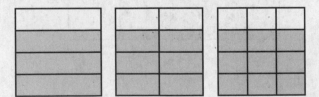

- ☐ $\frac{6}{6}$
- ☐ $\frac{2}{8}$
- ☐ $\frac{9}{12}$
- ☐ $\frac{6}{8}$
- ☐ $\frac{1}{2}$

17. Select all the pairs that are equivalent fractions. Use the area models to help.

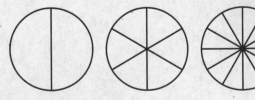

- ☐ $\frac{1}{6}$, $\frac{3}{12}$
- ☐ $\frac{2}{6}$, $\frac{4}{12}$
- ☐ $\frac{3}{6}$, $\frac{1}{2}$
- ☐ $\frac{1}{6}$, $\frac{6}{12}$
- ☐ $\frac{6}{6}$, $\frac{12}{12}$

Practice Video Tools Games

Additional Practice 8-2
Equivalent Fractions: Number Lines

Another Look!

You can write equivalent fractions for a point shown on a number line.

0   1

Label the number line in two different ways.

$\frac{1}{6}$ $\frac{2}{6}$ $\frac{3}{6}$ $\frac{4}{6}$ $\frac{5}{6}$

0   $\frac{1}{12}$ $\frac{2}{12}$ $\frac{3}{12}$ $\frac{4}{12}$ $\frac{5}{12}$ $\frac{6}{12}$ $\frac{7}{12}$ $\frac{8}{12}$ $\frac{9}{12}$ $\frac{10}{12}$ $\frac{11}{12}$ 1

The point is at $\frac{4}{6}$.

The point is at $\frac{8}{12}$.

$\frac{4}{6} = \frac{8}{12}$

$\frac{4}{6}$ and $\frac{8}{12}$ are equivalent fractions.

Equivalent fractions represent the same fractional amount of the same whole or same-sized wholes.

For **1–6**, write two fractions for the point on each number line.

1.

0   1

2.
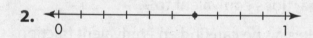
0   1

3.
0   1

4.
0   1

5.
0   1

6.
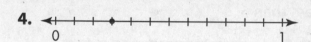
0   1

7. Are $\frac{3}{8}$ and $\frac{3}{4}$ equivalent fractions? Draw a number line to decide.

8. Draw a number line to show $\frac{1}{4}$ and $\frac{2}{8}$ are equivalent.

9. Mike says he can find a fraction equivalent to $\frac{1}{10}$, even though $\frac{1}{10}$ is a unit fraction. Is Mike correct? Explain.

10. **Algebra** There are 267 students and 21 adults going on a school trip. An equal number of people will ride on each bus. If there are 9 buses, how many people will ride on each bus? Write and solve equations.

11. Point X is at $\frac{2}{3}$ on a number line. On the same number line, point Y is the same distance from 0 as point X, but has a numerator of 8. What is the denominator of the fraction at point Y? Draw a number line to model the problem.

12. **Higher Order Thinking** A recipe calls for $\frac{1}{4}$ cup of flour. Carter only has a measuring cup that holds $\frac{1}{8}$ cup. How can Carter measure the flour he needs for his recipe?

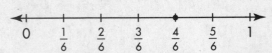

13. Monty is using a number line to find fractions equivalent to $\frac{4}{6}$.

    He says he can find an equivalent fraction with a denominator greater than 6 and an equivalent fraction with a denominator less than 6.

    You can further divide or relabel the number line to find equivalent fractions.

Part A

Write to explain how Monty can use the number line to find an equivalent fraction with a denominator greater than 6.

Part B

Write to explain how Monty can use the number line to find an equivalent fraction with a denominator less than 6.

Name _____

Another Look!

Use division to find two fractions equivalent to $\frac{8}{12}$.

To find an equivalent fraction, divide the numerator and denominator by any common factor other than 1.

$$\frac{8}{12} \div \frac{2}{2} = \frac{4}{6} \qquad \frac{8}{12} \div \frac{4}{4} = \frac{2}{3}$$

$\frac{8}{12}$, $\frac{4}{6}$, and $\frac{2}{3}$ are equivalent fractions.

For **1–8**, fill in the missing numbers to find equivalent fractions.

1. $\frac{5 \div 5}{10 \div 5} = \frac{\square}{\square}$

2. $\frac{2 \div 2}{12 \div 2} = \frac{\square}{\square}$

3. $\frac{12 \div 3}{6 \div 3} = \frac{\square}{\square}$

4. $\frac{40 \div 10}{100 \div 10} = \frac{\square}{\square}$

5. $\frac{25 \div \square}{100 \div \square} = \frac{\square}{4}$

6. $\frac{8 \div \square}{12 \div \square} = \frac{2}{\square}$

7. $\frac{70 \div \square}{100 \div \square} = \frac{7}{\square}$

8. $\frac{18 \div \square}{10 \div \square} = \frac{9}{\square}$

For **9–16**, find an equivalent fraction for each given fraction.

9. $\frac{75}{100}$

10. $\frac{4}{10}$

11. $\frac{10}{12}$

12. $\frac{200}{100}$

13. $\frac{24}{100}$

14. $\frac{60}{12}$

15. $\frac{84}{100}$

16. $\frac{70}{10}$

For **17–24**, divide to find two equivalent fractions.

17. $\frac{500}{100}$

18. $\frac{4}{12}$

19. $\frac{30}{10}$

20. $\frac{60}{100}$

21. $\frac{50}{10}$

22. $\frac{6}{12}$

23. $\frac{12}{8}$

24. $\frac{18}{6}$

25. What fraction of the game spinner is dark gray? Write two equivalent fractions.

26. Solve this number riddle:
I am an odd number.
I am less than 100.
The sum of my digits is 12.
I am a multiple of 15.

What number am I?

27. It took Bob 55 minutes to clean the garage. How many seconds did it take Bob? There are 60 seconds in one minute.

28. Betty is canning 104 pears and 126 apples separately. Each jar holds 8 pears or 6 apples. How many jars does Betty need?

29. Critique Reasoning Laurie says summer is $\frac{1}{4}$ of the year. Maria says summer is $\frac{3}{12}$ of the year. Who is correct? Explain.

30. Higher Order Thinking Cindy is using division to write a fraction equivalent to $\frac{30}{100}$. She tried to divide the numerator and denominator by 3. She got stuck. What advice would you give her?

✅ **Assessment Practice**

31. Which equation is **NOT** true?

Ⓐ $\frac{10}{12} = \frac{5}{6}$

Ⓑ $\frac{69}{100} = \frac{6}{10}$

Ⓒ $\frac{10}{5} = \frac{200}{100}$

Ⓓ $\frac{12}{4} = \frac{6}{2}$

32. Four out of 12 pieces of fruit in the basket are apples. Select all the fractions below that are equivalent to the fraction of fruit that is apples.

☐ $\frac{3}{6}$

☐ $\frac{1}{3}$

☐ $\frac{2}{6}$

☐ $\frac{1}{4}$

☐ $\frac{1}{6}$

Practice   Video   Tools   Games

Another Look!

Compare $\frac{6}{8}$ and $\frac{5}{12}$.

One Way

Compare the fractions to $\frac{1}{2}$.

$\frac{6}{8} > \frac{1}{2}$ $\frac{5}{12} < \frac{1}{2}$

$\frac{6}{8} > \frac{5}{12}$

Another Way

Compare the fractions to 0 and to 1.

$\frac{6}{8}$ is closer to 1 than to 0.

$\frac{5}{12}$ is closer to 0 than to 1.

$\frac{6}{8} > \frac{5}{12}$

Benchmarks can help you compare fractions.

For **1–6**, write three fractions that match each statement.

1. Fractions equal to $\frac{1}{2}$

2. Fractions less than $\frac{1}{2}$

3. Fractions greater than 1

4. Fractions closer to 1 than to 0

5. Fractions closer to 0 than to 1

6. Fractions greater than $\frac{1}{2}$

For **7–18**, compare using benchmark fractions or 1. Then write >, <, or =.

7. $\frac{3}{4} \bigcirc \frac{2}{10}$

8. $\frac{4}{12} \bigcirc \frac{7}{10}$

9. $\frac{5}{10} \bigcirc \frac{1}{2}$

10. $\frac{3}{8} \bigcirc \frac{6}{12}$

11. $\frac{7}{8} \bigcirc \frac{2}{5}$

12. $\frac{15}{12} \bigcirc \frac{5}{6}$

13. $\frac{5}{5} \bigcirc \frac{4}{4}$

14. $\frac{4}{6} \bigcirc \frac{1}{3}$

15. $\frac{8}{10} \bigcirc \frac{3}{5}$

16. $\frac{5}{8} \bigcirc \frac{6}{12}$

17. $\frac{48}{12} \bigcirc \frac{10}{5}$

18. $\frac{9}{12} \bigcirc \frac{5}{6}$

19. Write three fractions that are greater than $\frac{1}{2}$ but less than 1.

20. **Critique Reasoning** Mary lives $\frac{6}{10}$ mile from school. Thad lives $\frac{9}{8}$ miles from school. Mary says Thad lives farther from school. Is she correct? Explain.

21. Mr. Phillips is mixing paint for his art class. How many 6-ounce bottles can he fill with the quantities of paint shown at the right? Explain.

Paint

64 ounces of blue

12 ounces of yellow

32 ounces of white

22. Sandra used benchmark fractions to describe some insects she collected. She said the ladybug is about $\frac{1}{4}$ inch long, and the cricket is about $\frac{2}{3}$ inch long. Which insect is longer?

23. **Higher Order Thinking** Austin said, "I know $\frac{1}{4}$ is less than $\frac{1}{2}$, so that means $\frac{3}{12}$ is less than $\frac{1}{2}$." Does Austin's reasoning make sense? Explain.

☑ **Assessment Practice**

24. Kiyo and Steven are tiling the floors in an office building. Kiyo tiled $\frac{3}{6}$ of the floor in one office, and Steven tiled $\frac{5}{12}$ of the floor in another office.

Write to explain how to use a benchmark fraction to determine who tiled a greater portion of a floor.

You can compare these fractions because the floors in each office are the same size.

Practice   Video   Tools   Games

Additional Practice 8-6
Compare Fractions

Another Look!

Compare $\frac{2}{3}$ and $\frac{1}{2}$.

One Way

Rename one or both fractions so they both have the same denominator.

Rename both $\frac{2}{3}$ and $\frac{1}{2}$.

$\frac{2}{3} = \frac{2 \times 2}{3 \times 2} = \frac{4}{6}$

$\frac{1}{2} = \frac{1 \times 3}{2 \times 3} = \frac{3}{6}$

$\frac{4}{6} > \frac{3}{6}$, so $\frac{2}{3} > \frac{1}{2}$.

Another Way

Rename one or both fractions so they both have the same numerator.

Leave $\frac{2}{3}$ alone. Rename $\frac{1}{2}$.

$\frac{1}{2} = \frac{1 \times 2}{2 \times 2} = \frac{2}{4}$

$\frac{2}{3} > \frac{2}{4}$, so $\frac{2}{3} > \frac{1}{2}$.

When two fractions have the same numerator, the one with the lesser denominator is the greater fraction.

For **1–16**, find equivalent fractions to compare. Then write >, <, or =.

1. $\frac{5}{6} \bigcirc \frac{2}{3}$

2. $\frac{1}{5} \bigcirc \frac{2}{8}$

3. $\frac{9}{10} \bigcirc \frac{3}{4}$

4. $\frac{3}{4} \bigcirc \frac{2}{8}$

5. $\frac{7}{8} \bigcirc \frac{1}{2}$

6. $\frac{2}{5} \bigcirc \frac{2}{6}$

7. $\frac{1}{3} \bigcirc \frac{3}{8}$

8. $\frac{2}{10} \bigcirc \frac{3}{5}$

9. $\frac{8}{10} \bigcirc \frac{3}{4}$

10. $\frac{3}{8} \bigcirc \frac{9}{12}$

11. $\frac{2}{3} \bigcirc \frac{10}{12}$

12. $\frac{7}{8} \bigcirc \frac{3}{4}$

13. $\frac{3}{4} \bigcirc \frac{7}{8}$

14. $\frac{2}{4} \bigcirc \frac{4}{8}$

15. $\frac{6}{8} \bigcirc \frac{8}{12}$

16. $\frac{1}{3} \bigcirc \frac{4}{8}$

For **17–18**, use the table at the right. The same number of students attended school each day.

17. Did more students buy lunch on Thursday or on Wednesday?

18. Did more students buy lunch on Monday or on Friday?

Day	Fraction of Students Buying Lunch
Monday	$\frac{1}{2}$
Tuesday	$\frac{2}{5}$
Wednesday	$\frac{3}{4}$
Thursday	$\frac{5}{8}$
Friday	$\frac{4}{6}$

DATA

19. **Number Sense** Explain how you know $\frac{21}{100}$ is greater than $\frac{1}{5}$.

20. An orange was divided into 10 equal sections. Lily ate 4 sections. Manny and Emma ate the remaining sections. What fraction of the orange did Manny and Emma eat?

21. Which is longer, $\frac{1}{4}$ of line A or $\frac{1}{4}$ of line B? Explain.

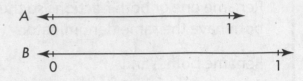

22. **Critique Reasoning** James says $\frac{5}{5}$ is greater than $\frac{9}{10}$. Is James correct? Explain.

23. Write 3 fractions with unlike denominators that are greater than the fraction shown below.

24. Ann works at a store in the mall and earns a wage of $8 an hour. She earns $10 an hour if she works on the weekends. Last week she worked 24 hours during the week and 16 hours on the weekend. How much did Ann earn last week?

25. **Higher Order Thinking** Four friends each ordered individual pizzas at a restaurant. Suzy ate $\frac{3}{8}$ of her pizza. Ethan ate $\frac{3}{5}$ of his pizza. Tenaya ate $\frac{4}{6}$ of her pizza. Sam ate $\frac{1}{3}$ of his pizza. Who ate more than half of their pizza? less than half?

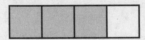
Assessment Practice

26. Select all the correct comparisons.

☐ $\frac{10}{12} > \frac{5}{6}$

☐ $\frac{6}{8} = \frac{3}{4}$

☐ $\frac{1}{8} > \frac{1}{10}$

☐ $\frac{9}{10} < \frac{4}{5}$

☐ $\frac{1}{100} > \frac{1}{10}$

27. Select all the fractions that are greater than $\frac{8}{12}$.

☐ $\frac{6}{6}$

☐ $\frac{50}{100}$

☐ $\frac{2}{4}$

☐ $\frac{5}{6}$

☐ $\frac{4}{6}$

Name _____

Another Look!

Gina and her brother Don made cornbread in equal-sized pans. Gina ate $\frac{1}{4}$ pan of cornbread. Don ate $\frac{3}{8}$ pan.

Tell how you can construct an argument to justify the conjecture that Don ate more cornbread.

- I can decide if the conjecture makes sense to me.

- I can use drawings and numbers to explain my reasoning.

When you construct arguments, you use drawings and numbers to explain.

One Way

I can draw a picture of two equal-sized wholes to show that Don ate more cornbread.

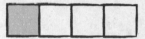   

$\frac{1}{4} < \frac{3}{8}$
Don ate more cornbread.

Another Way

I can use common denominators to compare $\frac{1}{4}$ and $\frac{3}{8}$. $\frac{1}{4}$ is equivalent to $\frac{2}{8}$.

Then I can compare the numerators of $\frac{2}{8}$ and $\frac{3}{8}$. Because the denominators are the same and $\frac{3}{8}$ has the greater numerator, $\frac{3}{8} > \frac{2}{8}$. Don ate more cornbread.

1. **Construct Arguments** A human usually has 20 baby teeth, which are replaced by 32 adult teeth. Raul lost 8 of his baby teeth. Raul said he lost $\frac{4}{10}$ of his baby teeth. Ana said Raul lost $\frac{2}{5}$ of his baby teeth. Which of these conjectures are true? Construct an argument to justify your answer.

Remember, a good argument is correct, simple, complete, and easy to understand.

2. **Construct Arguments** Trip has 15 coins worth 95 cents. Four of the coins are each worth twice as much as the rest. Construct a math argument to justify the conjecture that Trip has 11 nickels and 4 dimes.

Animal Weight and Food

Molly claims the animal listed in the table that weighs the most eats the most. She also claims that the animal that weighs the least, eats the least.

Animal	Weight	Food Eaten
Caribou	$\frac{7}{10}$ ton	12 pounds a day
Giraffe	$\frac{7}{8}$ ton	100 pounds a day
Panda	$\frac{1}{4}$ ton	301 pounds a week
Siberian Tiger	$\frac{1}{3}$ ton	55 pounds a day

3. **Make Sense and Persevere** Which animal eats the most? Explain.

4. **Construct Arguments** Does the animal that eats the most weigh more than the other animals? Explain, including how you made each comparison.

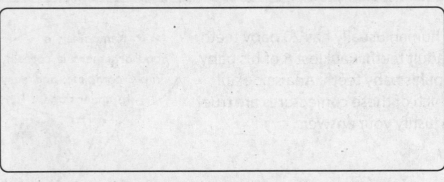

Remember, you can use words, objects, drawings, or diagrams when you construct an argument.

5. **Critique Reasoning** Explain whether or not you agree with Molly's claim.

6. **Reasoning** The caribou eats the least. Does it weigh the least? Explain.

Name _____

Another Look!

Eight friends went out to lunch. Four of them had pizza. Two had hamburgers and two had soup. What fraction of the group had either pizza or soup?

You can use a circle fraction model to add fractions.

Divide a circle into eighths to represent each of the 8 people in the group.	Four people had pizza. Shade 4 of the sections to represent $\frac{4}{8}$.	Count the number of $\frac{1}{8}$ sections. There are six $\frac{1}{8}$ sections shaded. So, $\frac{6}{8}$ of the group had either pizza or soup.
	Two people had soup. Shade 2 more sections to represent $\frac{2}{8}$. 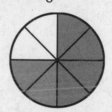	$\frac{4}{8} + \frac{2}{8} = \frac{6}{8}$ Add the numerators. Then write the sum over the like denominator.

For **1–12**, find each sum. Use a tool.

1. $\frac{1}{5} + \frac{1}{5}$

2. $\frac{4}{6} + \frac{1}{6}$

3. $\frac{5}{8} + \frac{2}{8}$

4. $\frac{2}{12} + \frac{2}{12}$

5. $\frac{2}{5} + \frac{3}{5}$

6. $\frac{2}{10} + \frac{3}{10}$

7. $\frac{5}{8} + \frac{3}{8}$

8. $\frac{3}{10} + \frac{1}{10}$

9. $\frac{3}{4} + \frac{1}{4}$

10. $\frac{5}{10} + \frac{4}{10}$

11. $\frac{1}{6} + \frac{1}{6} + \frac{1}{6}$

12. $\frac{1}{12} + \frac{5}{12} + \frac{2}{12}$

13. Critique Reasoning When Jared found $\frac{1}{5} + \frac{2}{5}$, he wrote the sum $\frac{3}{10}$. Is Jared correct? Explain.

14. Higher Order Thinking Leah wrote 2 different fractions with the same denominator. Both fractions were less than 1. Can their sum equal 1? Can their sum be greater than 1? Explain.

15. Sasha has a box of antique letters. She wants to give an equal number of letters to each of her 5 friends. How many antique letters will each friend receive?

There are 130 antique letters in the box.

16. Sandy made 8 friendship bracelets. She gave $\frac{1}{8}$ to her best friend and $\frac{5}{8}$ to her friends on the tennis team. Write and solve an equation to find the fraction of her bracelets, b, Sandy gave away.

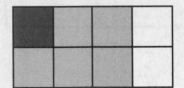

17. Draw a number line to show $\frac{2}{3} + \frac{2}{3}$.

---

18. Billy did $\frac{1}{6}$ of his homework on Friday. He did $\frac{1}{6}$ more on Saturday. Billy still had $\frac{4}{6}$ to finish. How much of his homework did Billy do on Friday and Saturday?

Ⓐ $\frac{2}{6}$

Ⓒ $\frac{4}{6}$

Ⓑ $\frac{3}{6}$

Ⓓ $\frac{5}{6}$

19. Roberto shares a bag of almonds with 2 friends. He shares $\frac{1}{8}$ bag with Jeremy and $\frac{2}{8}$ bag with Emily. He eats $\frac{3}{8}$ of the almonds himself. What fraction of the almonds do Roberto and his friends eat?

Ⓐ $\frac{1}{12}$

Ⓒ $\frac{6}{8}$

Ⓑ $\frac{3}{8}$

Ⓓ $\frac{7}{8}$

Name _____

Another Look!

Shannon wants to use $\frac{5}{8}$ of her garden space to plant petunias and marigolds. How can Shannon use the available space?

1				
$\frac{1}{8}$	$\frac{1}{8}$	$\frac{1}{8}$	$\frac{1}{8}$	$\frac{1}{8}$

Write $\frac{5}{8}$ as the sum of fractions in two different ways.

$$\frac{5}{8} = \frac{1}{8} + \frac{4}{8} \qquad \frac{5}{8} = \frac{2}{8} + \frac{3}{8}$$

Shannon could use $\frac{1}{8}$ of the space for petunias and $\frac{4}{8}$ for marigolds, or she could use $\frac{2}{8}$ of the space for petunias and $\frac{3}{8}$ for marigolds.

There are more than two solutions to this problem.

For **1–8**, decompose each fraction or mixed number in two different ways. Use a tool if needed.

1. $\frac{4}{8} =$

   $\frac{4}{8} =$

2. $\frac{7}{10} =$

   $\frac{7}{10} =$

3. $\frac{4}{5} =$

   $\frac{4}{5} =$

4. $\frac{3}{10} =$

   $\frac{3}{10} =$

5. $1\frac{1}{4} =$

   $1\frac{1}{4} =$

6. $2\frac{2}{3} =$

   $2\frac{2}{3} =$

Challenge yourself! Include ways that break a fraction or mixed number into more than two parts.

7. $1\frac{3}{5} =$

   $1\frac{3}{5} =$

8. $1\frac{1}{2} =$

   $1\frac{1}{2} =$

9. Yvonne ran $\frac{3}{8}$ of the race before stopping for water. She wants to stop for water one more time before finishing the race. List two ways Yvonne can do this.

$\frac{1}{8}$	$\frac{1}{8}$	$\frac{1}{8}$	$\frac{1}{8}$	$\frac{1}{8}$	$\frac{1}{8}$	$\frac{1}{8}$	$\frac{1}{8}$

10. Reasoning A teacher noticed $\frac{5}{8}$ of the students were wearing either blue shorts or white shorts. Write two different ways this could be done.

11. Connie made $1\frac{1}{3}$ pounds of trail mix for a hike. Is there a way Connie can break up the trail mix into four bags? Explain.

12. Jo's Donut Express earned $4,378 at a festival by selling chocolate or vanilla donuts for $2 each. If they sold 978 chocolate donuts, how many vanilla donuts did they sell?

13. Higher Order Thinking Mark decomposed $\frac{5}{6}$ into three fractions. None of the fractions had a denominator of 6. What fractions might Mark have used? Remember, you can use equivalent fractions.

☑ **Assessment Practice**

14. Select all the ways that decompose $\frac{9}{10}$. Use a fraction model if needed.

☐ $\frac{4}{10} + \frac{5}{10}$

☐ $\frac{3}{10} + \frac{1}{10} + \frac{1}{10} + \frac{1}{10} + \frac{1}{10} + \frac{1}{10}$

☐ $\frac{3}{10} + \frac{7}{10}$

☐ $\frac{1}{10} + \frac{1}{10} + \frac{3}{10} + \frac{4}{10}$

☐ $\frac{4}{10} + \frac{2}{10} + \frac{2}{10} + \frac{1}{10}$

15. Select all the ways that decompose $1\frac{3}{8}$. Use a fraction model if needed.

☐ $\frac{3}{8} + \frac{3}{8} + \frac{3}{8} + \frac{2}{8}$

☐ $1 + \frac{3}{8}$

☐ $\frac{8}{8} + \frac{3}{8}$

☐ $\frac{5}{8} + \frac{5}{8} + \frac{1}{8}$

☐ $1 + \frac{1}{4} + \frac{2}{4}$

Practice Video Tools Games

Another Look!

Find $\frac{4}{8} + \frac{2}{8}$.

When you add fractions with like denominators, add the numerators and keep the denominators the same.

$\frac{4}{8} = \frac{1}{8} + \frac{1}{8} + \frac{1}{8} + \frac{1}{8}$ $\frac{2}{8} = \frac{1}{8} + \frac{1}{8}$

0 ———————————— 1

$\frac{4}{8} + \frac{2}{8} = \frac{4+2}{6} = \frac{6}{8}$

For **1–18**, find each sum. Use drawings or fraction strips as needed.

1. $\frac{1}{3} + \frac{1}{3}$

2. $\frac{3}{10} + \frac{6}{10}$

3. $\frac{5}{12} + \frac{2}{12}$

4. $\frac{3}{12} + \frac{7}{12}$

5. $\frac{5}{10} + \frac{3}{10}$

6. $\frac{2}{8} + \frac{4}{8}$

7. $\frac{7}{10} + \frac{3}{10}$

8. $\frac{1}{8} + \frac{6}{8}$

9. $\frac{1}{10} + \frac{5}{10}$

10. $\frac{4}{5} + \frac{1}{5}$

11. $\frac{2}{8} + \frac{6}{8}$

12. $\frac{6}{10} + 0$

13. $\frac{1}{5} + \frac{2}{5} + \frac{4}{5}$

14. $\frac{2}{8} + \frac{1}{8} + \frac{12}{8}$

15. $\frac{2}{6} + \frac{10}{6}$

16. $\frac{20}{100} + \frac{25}{100} + \frac{25}{100}$

17. $\frac{2}{10} + \frac{6}{10} + \frac{1}{10}$

18. $\frac{10}{10} + \frac{10}{10} + \frac{10}{10}$

For **19–21**, use the table at the right.

19. What fraction of the students voted for fruit juice or soda?

20. Which two beverages have a sum of $\frac{5}{8}$ of the student votes?

21. **Model with Math** Write and solve an equation to find what fraction of the students, f, voted for fruit juice or water.

Favorite Beverage	Fraction of Student Votes
Iced Tea	$\frac{3}{8}$
Fruit Juice	$\frac{2}{8}$
Water	$\frac{1}{8}$
Soda	$\frac{2}{8}$

DATA

22. A bus traveled 336 miles in 7 hours. It traveled the same number of miles each hour. If the bus continues at the same number of miles per hour, how many miles will the bus travel in 15 hours? Explain.

23. **Higher Order Thinking** How can you add $\frac{3}{10}$ and $\frac{2}{5}$? Explain.

Think about a different name for $\frac{2}{5}$.

✅ **Assessment Practice**

24. Match each expression with its sum.

	$\frac{4}{8}$	$\frac{6}{8}$	$\frac{7}{8}$	$1\frac{1}{8}$
$\frac{5}{8} + \frac{1}{8}$	☐	☐	☐	☐
$\frac{6}{8} + \frac{3}{8}$	☐	☐	☐	☐
$\frac{3}{8} + \frac{4}{8}$	☐	☐	☐	☐
$\frac{2}{8} + \frac{2}{8}$	☐	☐	☐	☐

25. In Fred's catering order, $\frac{5}{12}$ of the lunches are sandwiches, $\frac{2}{12}$ are salads, and $\frac{4}{12}$ are pastas. Which equation can be used to find c, the fraction of the catering order that is sandwiches or salads?

Ⓐ $c = \frac{5}{12} + \frac{4}{12}$

Ⓑ $c = \frac{5}{12} + \frac{2}{12}$

Ⓒ $c = \frac{2}{12} + \frac{4}{12}$

Ⓓ $c = \frac{5}{12} + \frac{2}{12} + \frac{4}{12}$

118 **Topic 9** | Lesson 9-3

Practice Video Tools Games

Another Look!

Kimberly cut a pizza into 10 equal slices. She ate two of the slices. What fraction of the pizza is left? Remember, $\frac{10}{10} = 1$ whole pizza.

Step 1

Divide a circle into tenths to show the pizza cut into 10 slices.

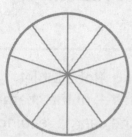

Step 2

Take away the 2 slices or $\frac{2}{10}$ of the pizza that Kimberly ate.

Step 3

Count the remaining slices and write the subtraction.

$$\frac{10}{10} - \frac{2}{10} = \frac{8}{10}$$

$\frac{8}{10}$ of the pizza is left.

For **1–12**, find each difference. Use fraction strips or other tools as needed.

1. $\frac{3}{5} - \frac{2}{5}$

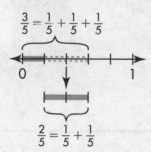

$\frac{3}{5} = \frac{1}{5} + \frac{1}{5} + \frac{1}{5}$

$\frac{2}{5} = \frac{1}{5} + \frac{1}{5}$

2. $\frac{7}{10} - \frac{3}{10}$

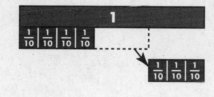

3. $\frac{4}{4} - \frac{2}{4}$

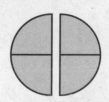

4. $\frac{8}{10} - \frac{5}{10}$

5. $\frac{6}{6} - \frac{3}{6}$

6. $\frac{11}{12} - \frac{7}{12}$

7. $\frac{5}{6} - \frac{2}{6}$

8. $\frac{4}{8} - \frac{2}{8}$

9. $\frac{11}{12} - \frac{8}{12}$

10. $\frac{9}{8} - \frac{2}{8}$

11. $\frac{24}{4} - \frac{18}{4}$

12. $\frac{30}{10} - \frac{20}{10}$

13. Eddie noticed that out of 10 students, 1 student was wearing brown shoes, and 7 students were wearing black shoes. What fraction of students were **NOT** wearing brown or black shoes?

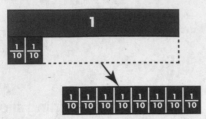

14. **Make Sense and Persevere** A marathon is a race that covers about 26 miles. Cindy ran 5 miles before taking her first water break. Then she ran another 7 miles to get to her next water break. After 6 more miles, she took her last water break. About how much farther does Cindy have until she reaches the finish line?

15. **Algebra** Jeffrey has already run $\frac{3}{8}$ of the race. What fraction of the race does Jeffrey have left? Write and solve an equation.

16. **Higher Order Thinking** Rob's tablet is fully charged. He uses $\frac{1}{12}$ of the charge playing games, $\frac{5}{12}$ of the charge reading, and $\frac{3}{12}$ completing homework. What fraction of the charge remains on Rob's tablet?

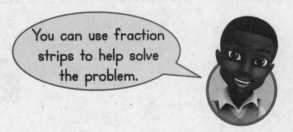

You can use fraction strips to help solve the problem.

Assessment Practice

17. Which subtraction problem has a difference of $\frac{2}{5}$?

Ⓐ $\frac{3}{5} - \frac{2}{5}$

Ⓑ $\frac{3}{6} - \frac{1}{2}$

Ⓒ $\frac{4}{5} - \frac{1}{5}$

Ⓓ $\frac{5}{5} - \frac{3}{5}$

18. Which subtraction problem has a difference of $\frac{2}{3}$?

Ⓐ $\frac{7}{3} - \frac{5}{3}$

Ⓑ $\frac{5}{3} - \frac{2}{3}$

Ⓒ $\frac{2}{3} - \frac{1}{3}$

Ⓓ $\frac{8}{3} - \frac{7}{3}$

Name _____

Practice   Video   Tools   Games

Subtract Fractions with Like Denominators

Another Look!

Flora has $\frac{10}{8}$ cups of flour. She uses $\frac{6}{8}$ cup to make dough. How much flour, n, does Flora have left?

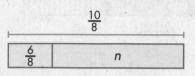

Subtract the numerators. Write the difference over the like denominator.

$n = \frac{10}{8} - \frac{6}{8}$, $n = \frac{4}{8}$

Flora has $\frac{4}{8}$ cup flour left.

Bar diagrams can help you represent the problem.

For **1–10**, subtract the fractions.

1. $\frac{6}{8} - \frac{3}{8}$

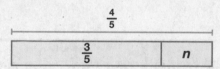

2. $\frac{4}{6} - \frac{1}{6}$

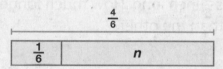

3. $\frac{4}{5} - \frac{3}{5}$

4. $\frac{3}{6} - \frac{1}{6}$

5. $\frac{97}{100} - \frac{40}{100}$

6. $\frac{5}{8} - \frac{1}{8}$

7. $\frac{10}{10} - \frac{9}{10}$

8. $\frac{17}{12} - \frac{5}{12}$

9. $\frac{33}{100} - \frac{4}{100}$

10. $\frac{50}{100} - \frac{10}{100}$

11. Model with Math An engineer says a pipe should be $\frac{7}{10}$ centimeter long. The pipe is $\frac{9}{10}$ centimeter long. How much of the pipe needs to be cut off? Write an equation.

$\frac{9}{10}$ centimeter

n	$\frac{7}{10}$

12. A mosaic wall is divided into 100 equal sections. If 30 sections are reserved for orange tiles and 40 sections are reserved for blue tiles, what fraction of the mosaic wall is left for other colors?

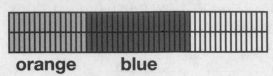

orange   blue

13. Number Sense Jonah is thinking of a 2-digit number. It is a multiple of 6 and 12. It is a factor of 108. The sum of its digits is 9. What number is Jonah thinking of?

14. In a bag of 100 balloons, 12 are red and 13 are green. What fraction of the balloons in the bag are **NOT** red or green?

15. enVision® STEM Mary saw two poison dart frogs. One was $\frac{7}{8}$ inch long and the other was $\frac{5}{8}$ inch long. How much longer was one than the other?

16. Higher Order Thinking Diego compared the differences for $\frac{10}{10} - \frac{1}{10}$ and $\frac{100}{100} - \frac{10}{100}$. He said the differences both equal $\frac{9}{10}$. Is Diego correct? Explain.

17. Teri has $\frac{9}{10}$ kilogram of oranges. She ate $\frac{2}{10}$ kilogram. How much of a kilogram remains?

18. Conner ate $\frac{7}{12}$ of his foot-long sandwich. Write and solve an equation to find s, the part of the sandwich that is left.

$\frac{12}{12}$

$\frac{7}{12}$	s

Name _____

Practice Video Tools Games

Another Look!

You can use a tool such as fraction strips or number lines to show the addition and subtraction of mixed numbers.

Use a number line to find $1\frac{7}{8} + 2\frac{3}{8}$.

Use a number line for eighths. Start at $1\frac{7}{8}$.

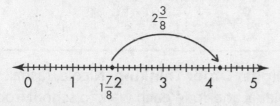

To add, move $2\frac{3}{8}$ to the right.

Write the sum as a fraction or a mixed number.

So, $1\frac{7}{8} + 2\frac{3}{8} = 4\frac{2}{8}$.

Use fraction strips to find $2\frac{1}{5} - 1\frac{2}{5}$.

Model the number you are subtracting from, $2\frac{1}{5}$.

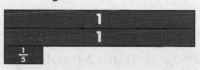

Rename $2\frac{1}{5}$ as $1\frac{6}{5}$. Cross out one whole and $\frac{2}{5}$ to show subtracting $1\frac{2}{5}$.

Write the difference as a fraction.

So, $2\frac{1}{5} - 1\frac{2}{5} = \frac{4}{5}$.

For **1–9**, use a tool to find each sum or difference.

1. $3\frac{1}{2} + 1\frac{1}{2}$

2. $3\frac{3}{4} - 2\frac{1}{4}$

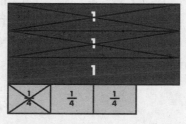

3. $1\frac{3}{4} + 1\frac{3}{4}$

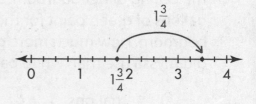

4. $3\frac{4}{5} - 1\frac{2}{5}$

5. $5\frac{2}{6} + 3\frac{5}{6}$

6. $10\frac{2}{8} - 7\frac{5}{8}$

7. $2\frac{5}{12} + 4\frac{3}{12}$

8. $12\frac{1}{3} - 5\frac{2}{3}$

9. $2\frac{2}{4} + 6\frac{3}{4}$

For **10–12**, use the table at the right.

10. How many inches longer is a Hercules beetle than a ladybug?

11. What is the difference between the largest and the smallest stag beetles?

12. How long are a Hercules beetle and a ladybug combined?

Beetles by Length	
Beetle	**Length in Inches**
Hercules beetle	$6\frac{3}{4}$
Ladybug	$\frac{1}{4}$
Stag beetle	$2\frac{1}{8}$ to $2\frac{4}{8}$

13. Stan needs 90 points to get a passing grade in class. He already has 6 points. If each book report is worth 7 points, what is the fewest number of book reports Stan can do and still pass the class?

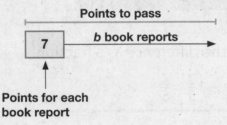

Points to pass

7   *b* book reports

Points for each book report

14. **Higher Order Thinking** Nicole, Tasha, Maria, and Joan each walk to school from home. Nicole walks $1\frac{11}{12}$ miles. Tasha walks $2\frac{1}{12}$ miles. Maria walks $1\frac{7}{12}$ miles. Joan walks $2\frac{2}{12}$ miles. How can you find how much farther Joan walks to school than Maria?

✓ **Assessment Practice**

15. Alyssa used $1\frac{2}{3}$ gallons of white paint for the ceiling of her bedroom. She used $3\frac{1}{3}$ gallons of green paint for the walls of her bedroom. How much more green paint did Alyssa use than white paint?

   Ⓐ $1\frac{1}{3}$ gallons

   Ⓑ $1\frac{2}{3}$ gallons

   Ⓒ   2 gallons

   Ⓓ $2\frac{1}{3}$ gallons

16. Jerome's rain gauge showed $3\frac{9}{10}$ centimeters of rain fell last month. This month, the rain gauge measured $5\frac{3}{10}$ centimeters. Which equation can be used to find r, how many more centimeters of rain fell this month than last month?

   Ⓐ $r = 5\frac{3}{10} + 3\frac{9}{10}$

   Ⓑ $r = 5\frac{3}{10} + 3\frac{6}{10}$

   Ⓒ $r = 5\frac{3}{10} - 3\frac{6}{10}$

   Ⓓ $r = 5\frac{3}{10} - 3\frac{9}{10}$

Practice Video Tools Games

Another Look!

Randy played basketball for $2\frac{5}{6}$ hours on Saturday.
He played for $1\frac{3}{6}$ hours on Sunday. How many hours
did Randy play basketball on the weekend?

Add Mixed Numbers

a. Add the fractions.

b. Add the whole numbers.

c. Write the fraction as a
mixed number.

$$2\frac{5}{6}$$
$$+\ 1\frac{3}{6}$$
$$\overline{3\frac{8}{6}} = 4\frac{2}{6}$$

$$3\frac{8}{6} = 3 + \frac{6}{6} + \frac{2}{6} = 4\frac{2}{6}$$

Randy played basketball for $4\frac{2}{6}$ hours on
the weekend.

Add Fractions

a. Write the mixed
numbers as fractions.

b. Add the fractions.

c. Write the fraction
as a mixed number.

$$2\frac{5}{6} = \frac{17}{6}$$
$$+\ 1\frac{3}{6} = +\frac{9}{6}$$
$$\overline{\frac{26}{6}} = 4\frac{2}{6}$$

$$\frac{26}{6} = \frac{6}{6} + \frac{6}{6} + \frac{6}{6} + \frac{6}{6} + \frac{2}{6} = 4\frac{2}{6}$$

You can add mixed numbers
with like denominators using
properties of operations.

For **1–12**, find each sum by adding mixed numbers or adding equivalent fractions.

1. $2\frac{10}{12}$
   $+ 3\frac{3}{12}$

2. $1\frac{3}{8}$
   $+ 3\frac{6}{8}$

3. $5\frac{4}{10}$
   $+ 4\frac{2}{10}$

4. $10\frac{2}{6}$
   $+\ \ \frac{3}{6}$

5. $3\frac{3}{12} + 6\frac{8}{12}$

6. $1\frac{2}{5} + 3\frac{1}{5}$

7. $2\frac{10}{12} + 3\frac{9}{12}$

8. $2\frac{2}{6} + 3\frac{5}{6}$

9. $4\frac{3}{4} + 2\frac{2}{4}$

10. $1\frac{9}{10} + 3\frac{2}{10}$

11. $1\frac{8}{12} + 3\frac{5}{12}$

12. $1\frac{11}{12} + 2\frac{5}{12}$

13. 🄰🄱 **Vocabulary** Use the vocabulary words *mixed number* and *fractions* to complete the sentence.

When adding mixed numbers, you can first add the _____, then add the whole numbers. Finally, you write the

_____.

14. Construct Arguments Explain one strategy for finding $2\frac{2}{5} + 1\frac{2}{5}$.

15. Ruth needs $2\frac{1}{4}$ cups of flour for one cake recipe and $2\frac{3}{4}$ cups of flour for another cake recipe. If she makes both cakes, how much flour will Ruth use altogether?

16. A "stone" is an old unit of weight used in Ireland and England to measure potatoes. A stone is 14 pounds and 80 stones make up half of a "long ton." How many pounds is half of a long ton?

17. Higher Order Thinking Tirzah wants to put a fence around her garden. She has 22 yards of fence material. Does Tirzah have enough to go all the way around the garden? Explain.

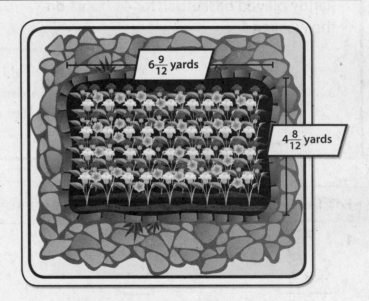

$6\frac{9}{12}$ yards

$4\frac{8}{12}$ yards

18. Pookie weighs $2\frac{7}{8}$ pounds. Rascal weighs $3\frac{3}{8}$ pounds. What is the total weight of both cats? Select all the correct ways to find the sum.

☐ $\frac{23}{8} + \frac{27}{8} = \frac{50}{8}$

☐ $(2 + 3) + \left(\frac{7}{8} + \frac{3}{8}\right)$

☐ $5 + \frac{10}{8}$

☐ $\frac{23}{8} + \frac{27}{8} = \frac{50}{16}$

☐ $5 + \frac{10}{16}$

19. Select all correct sums.

☐ $5\frac{1}{3} + 3\frac{1}{3} = 9\frac{2}{3}$

☐ $2\frac{4}{5} + 1\frac{3}{5} = 3\frac{2}{5}$

☐ $1\frac{7}{8} + 2\frac{7}{8} = 4\frac{6}{8}$

☐ $3\frac{4}{10} + 2\frac{8}{10} = 6\frac{2}{10}$

☐ $3\frac{5}{6} + 2\frac{4}{6} = 5\frac{4}{6}$

Practice · Video · Tools · Games

Another Look!

Janet grew a pumpkin that weighs $13\frac{3}{4}$ pounds and a melon that weighs $8\frac{2}{4}$ pounds. How much heavier is the pumpkin than the melon?

Subtract Mixed Numbers

$$13\frac{3}{4}$$
$$-\ 8\frac{2}{4}$$
$$\overline{5\frac{1}{4}}$$

a. Subtract the fractions. Rename whole numbers as fractions as needed.

b. Subtract the whole numbers.

The pumpkin is $5\frac{1}{4}$ pounds heavier than the melon.

Subtract Fractions

a. Write the mixed numbers as fractions.

b. Subtract the fractions.

c. Write the fraction as a mixed number.

$$\frac{21}{4} = \frac{20}{4} + \frac{1}{4} = 5\frac{1}{4}$$

$$13\frac{3}{4} = \frac{55}{4}$$
$$-\ 8\frac{2}{4} = -\frac{34}{4}$$
$$\overline{\frac{21}{4} = 5\frac{1}{4}}$$

You can subtract mixed numbers with like denominators more than one way.

For **1–16**, find each difference.

1. $10\frac{3}{4}$
$-\ 7\frac{1}{4}$

2. $7\frac{4}{6}$
$-\ 2\frac{3}{6}$

3. 3
$-\ 2\frac{2}{3}$

4. $7\frac{8}{12}$
$-\ 2\frac{3}{12}$

5. $5\frac{2}{6} - 2\frac{5}{6}$

6. $4\frac{1}{5} - 2\frac{3}{5}$

7. $4\frac{3}{12} - 1\frac{4}{12}$

8. $5\frac{2}{8} - 3\frac{7}{8}$

9. $8\frac{1}{4} - 7\frac{3}{4}$

10. $2\frac{9}{10} - 2\frac{5}{10}$

11. $6\frac{5}{6} - 5\frac{4}{6}$

12. $3 - 1\frac{3}{4}$

13. $6 - 2\frac{1}{2}$

14. $12\frac{6}{10} - 10$

15. $8\frac{1}{5} - 2\frac{2}{5}$

16. $7\frac{2}{6} - 2\frac{1}{6}$

17. (A-Z) **Vocabulary** Use a vocabulary word to complete the sentence.

A number that has a whole number part and a fractional part is a called a(n) _____.

18. Some of the world's smallest horses include: Thumbelina, who stands $17\frac{1}{4}$ inches tall; Black Beauty, who stands $18\frac{2}{4}$ inches tall; and Einstein, who stands 14 inches tall.

   a. How much taller is Black Beauty than Thumbelina?

   b. How much taller is Thumbelina than Einstein?

19. **Reasoning** If Carol hangs a picture using $\frac{3}{8}$ yard of a wire that is $1\frac{1}{8}$ yards long, how much wire will Carol have left?

20. Write 6,219 in expanded form.

21. **Higher Order Thinking** Some of the largest insects in the world include the Rhinoceros Beetle, the Giant Walking Stick, and the Giant Weta Beetle. How much longer is the Giant Walking Stick than the Rhinoceros Beetle and the Giant Weta Beetle combined?

Rhinoceros Beetle
$16\frac{7}{10}$ cm

Giant Walking Stick
$53\frac{3}{10}$ cm

Giant Weta Beetle
$8\frac{5}{10}$ cm

✓ **Assessment Practice**

22. Jessie has a board $5\frac{1}{12}$ feet long. She cuts off $3\frac{9}{12}$ feet. How much of the length is left?

   Ⓐ $1\frac{4}{12}$ feet

   Ⓑ $2\frac{8}{12}$ feet

   Ⓒ $2\frac{9}{12}$ feet

   Ⓓ $8\frac{10}{12}$ feet

23. Robyn ran $5\frac{3}{4}$ miles last week. She ran $4\frac{1}{4}$ miles this week. How many more miles did Robyn run last week than this week?

   Ⓐ $1\frac{1}{4}$ miles

   Ⓑ $1\frac{2}{4}$ miles

   Ⓒ $1\frac{3}{4}$ miles

   Ⓓ 10 miles

Practice   Video   Tools   Games

Another Look!

Tina built $\frac{1}{8}$ of a model airplane on Saturday and $\frac{4}{8}$ on Sunday. She built $\frac{3}{8}$ more on Monday. How much more of the model airplane did she build on the weekend than on the weekday?

Tell how you can use math to model the problem.

- I can use previously learned concepts and skills.

- I can use bar diagrams and equations to represent and solve this problem.

- I can decide if my results make sense.

> When you model with math, you use previously learned math to solve a problem.

Draw a bar diagram and write and solve equations.

$\frac{1}{8} + \frac{4}{8} = w, w = \frac{5}{8}$

$\frac{5}{8} - \frac{3}{8} = n$

$n = \frac{2}{8}$

$\frac{5}{8}$	
$\frac{3}{8}$	n

> Let w = how much Tina built on the weekend and n = how much more she built on the weekend than the weekday.

Tina built $\frac{2}{8}$ more of the model airplane on the weekend than on the weekday.

Model with Math

On Nick's playlist, $\frac{5}{12}$ of the songs are pop. What fraction of the songs, n, are **NOT** pop? Use Exercises 1–3 to answer the question.

1. How can you draw a picture and write an equation to represent the problem?

2. What previously learned math can you use to solve the problem?

3. What fraction of the songs on Nick's playlist are **NOT** pop?

Ian and Rachel each made a trail mix. The amounts of ingredients they have are shown. Ian used all of the coconut, dried cranberries, and dried bananas to make his trail mix. Rachel made 2 cups of trail mix containing all of the almonds, pumpkin seeds, and granola. How much trail mix did Ian make? How much more trail mix did Rachel make than Ian?

Trail Mix Ingredients
$\frac{3}{4}$ cup almonds
$\frac{1}{4}$ cup pumpkin seeds
$\frac{2}{4}$ cup coconut
$\frac{3}{4}$ cup dried cranberries
$1\frac{2}{4}$ cup walnuts
1 cup granola
$\frac{2}{4}$ cup dried bananas

4. **Make Sense and Persevere** What do you know, and what do you need to find?

5. **Use Appropriate Tools** What tools could you use to help solve this problem?

6. **Reasoning** How can you use bar diagrams to show how the quantities are related?

When you model with math, you use math to represent the problem.

7. **Make Sense and Persevere** Write and solve an equation to find how much trail mix Ian made.

8. **Reasoning** Write and solve an equation to find how much more trail mix Rachel made than Ian.

Name _____

Another Look!

Use fraction strips to show $\frac{5}{8}$ as a multiple of a unit fraction.

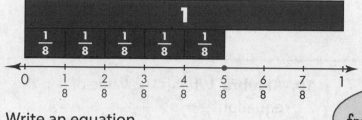

Write an equation.

$$\frac{5}{8} = \frac{1}{8} + \frac{1}{8} + \frac{1}{8} + \frac{1}{8} + \frac{1}{8}$$

$$\frac{5}{8} = 5 \times \frac{1}{8}$$

> You can write any fraction as a multiple of a unit fraction.

For **1–15**, write each fraction as a multiple of a unit fraction. Use a tool as needed.

1. $\frac{2}{4} = 2 \times \frac{\square}{4}$

$\frac{1}{4}$	$\frac{1}{4}$	$\frac{1}{4}$	$\frac{1}{4}$

2. $\frac{2}{6} = \square \times \frac{1}{6}$

$\frac{1}{6}$	$\frac{1}{6}$	$\frac{1}{6}$	$\frac{1}{6}$	$\frac{1}{6}$	$\frac{1}{6}$

3. $\frac{5}{2} = \square \times \frac{1}{2}$

$\frac{1}{2}$	$\frac{1}{2}$	$\frac{1}{2}$	$\frac{1}{2}$

$\frac{1}{2}$	$\frac{1}{2}$

4. $\frac{3}{3} = 3 \times \frac{1}{\square}$

5. $\frac{10}{8} = 10 \times \frac{\square}{8}$

6. $\frac{2}{5} = 2 \times \frac{1}{\square}$

7. $\frac{1}{6}$

8. $\frac{9}{5}$

9. $\frac{8}{3}$

10. $\frac{9}{10}$

11. $\frac{9}{12}$

12. $\frac{8}{10}$

13. $\frac{6}{3}$

14. $\frac{6}{8}$

15. $\frac{4}{12}$

16. Kevin is baking cookies. Each batch of cookies uses $\frac{1}{8}$ pound of butter. Kevin has $\frac{11}{8}$ pounds of butter. How many batches of cookies can Kevin make? Explain by writing $\frac{11}{8}$ as a multiple of $\frac{1}{8}$.

17. Students are painting a mural. So far, the mural is painted $\frac{4}{12}$ blue, $\frac{2}{12}$ red, and $\frac{3}{12}$ green. Write and solve an equation to find m, how much of the mural has been painted.

18. 🅐🅩 **Vocabulary** How can you tell if a fraction is a *unit fraction*?

19. **Algebra** What is the value of p in the equation $\frac{10}{6} = p \times \frac{1}{6}$?

20. **Look for Relationships** Mari packs the same number of oranges in each bag. How many oranges does Mari need to pack 9 bags? How can you determine the number of oranges Mari needs for 13 bags?

Number of Bags	3	5	7	9	11
Number of Oranges	9	15	21		33

21. **Higher Order Thinking** Katrina has $\frac{2}{3}$ of a gallon of ice cream. She uses $\frac{1}{6}$ gallon as a serving. How many servings does she have? Explain by writing $\frac{2}{3}$ as an equivalent fraction with a denominator of 6 and then writing the fraction as a multiple of $\frac{1}{6}$.

22. Which multiplication equation describes the fraction plotted on the number line?

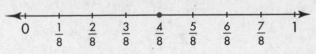

Ⓐ $\frac{4}{8} = 4 + \frac{1}{8}$

Ⓑ $\frac{4}{8} = 4 \times \frac{1}{8}$

Ⓒ $\frac{4}{8} = \frac{1}{8} + \frac{2}{8} + \frac{3}{8} + \frac{4}{8}$

Ⓓ $\frac{4}{8} = 8 \times \frac{1}{4}$

23. Which multiplication equation describes the fraction strips below?

Ⓐ $\frac{7}{10} = \frac{1}{10} + \frac{1}{10} + \frac{1}{10} + \frac{1}{10} + \frac{1}{10} + \frac{1}{10}$

Ⓑ $\frac{7}{10} = 7 \times \frac{1}{10}$

Ⓒ $\frac{6}{10} = 6 + \frac{1}{10}$

Ⓓ $\frac{6}{10} = 6 \times \frac{1}{10}$

Name _____

Video Practice Tools Games

Another Look!

Georgie walked $\frac{2}{3}$ mile to and from the gym. How many miles did Georgie walk?

Find $2 \times \frac{2}{3}$.

$$2 \times \frac{2}{3} = \frac{2}{3} + \frac{2}{3}$$
$$= \frac{4}{3}$$
$$= \frac{3}{3} + \frac{1}{3} = 1\frac{1}{3}$$

Georgie walked $1\frac{1}{3}$ miles.

You can use a number line and repeated addition to multiply fractions and whole numbers.

For **1–6**, write and solve a multiplication equation. Use drawings or number lines as needed.

1.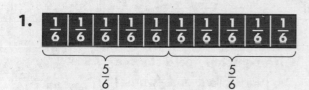

2.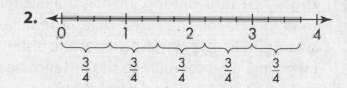

3.

4.

5. Calculate the distance Penny rides her bicycle if she rides $\frac{1}{4}$ mile each day for 5 days.

6. Calculate the distance Benjamin rides his scooter if he rides $\frac{3}{5}$ mile each day for 4 days.

7. At a play, 211 guests are seated on the main floor and 142 guests are seated in the balcony. If tickets for the main floor cost $7 and tickets for the balcony cost $5, how much was earned in ticket sales?

8. Audrey uses $\frac{5}{8}$ cup of fruit in each smoothie she makes. She makes 6 smoothies to share with her friends. How many cups of fruit does Audrey use?

$\frac{5}{8}$	$\frac{5}{8}$	$\frac{5}{8}$	$\frac{5}{8}$	$\frac{5}{8}$	$\frac{5}{8}$

9. Gabe is making 5 capes. He uses $\frac{2}{3}$ yard of fabric for each cape he makes. What is the total amount of fabric Gabe needs?

$\frac{2}{3}$	$\frac{2}{3}$	$\frac{2}{3}$	$\frac{2}{3}$	$\frac{2}{3}$

10. **Use Structure** Draw a picture to show how to find $4 \times \frac{3}{5}$.

11. **Higher Order Thinking** Mark is training for a mini triathlon. He rode his bike $\frac{3}{4}$ mile, ran $\frac{2}{4}$ mile, and swam $\frac{1}{4}$ mile each day. How does the distance he biked in 3 days compare to the distance he swam in 3 days? In 5 days? In 6 days? Why?

> You can use structure or draw a picture to compare the distances Mark biked and swam.

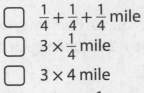

✓ Assessment Practice

12. Ronald rode the rollercoaster 3 times. The rollercoaster track is $\frac{1}{4}$ mile in length. Select all the expressions that tell how far Ronald rode in all. Use drawings or number lines as needed.

☐ $\frac{1}{4} + \frac{1}{4} + \frac{1}{4}$ mile
☐ $3 \times \frac{1}{4}$ mile
☐ 3×4 mile
☐ $4 + 3 \times \frac{1}{4}$ mile
☐ $\frac{3}{4}$ mile

13. Kurt swam across the lake and back. The lake is $\frac{4}{8}$ mile across. Select all the equations that can be used to find s, the total distance Kurt swam.

☐ $s = 2 \times \frac{4}{8}$
☐ $s = \frac{4}{8} + \frac{4}{8}$
☐ $s = 1$
☐ $s = 2 \times 8$
☐ $s = 2 + \frac{4}{8}$

Name _____

Another Look!

You can add, subtract, multiply, or divide measures of time to solve problems.

Add

Ann worked 5 years 7 months at her first job. She worked 3 years 3 months at her second job. How long did Ann work at her first and second jobs?

```
  5 years   7 months
+ 3 years   3 months
  8 years  10 months
```

Subtract

Ann worked $2\frac{4}{5}$ weeks in December and $4\frac{1}{5}$ weeks in January. How many more weeks did she work in January than December?

$$4\frac{1}{5} - 2\frac{4}{5} = 3\frac{6}{5} - 2\frac{4}{5} = 1\frac{2}{5} \text{ weeks}$$

Multiply

Ann worked 3 times longer at her fourth job than her third job. Ann worked $\frac{11}{12}$ year at her third job. How long did Ann work at her fourth job?

$$3 \times \frac{11}{12} = \frac{33}{12}$$
$$= \frac{12}{12} + \frac{12}{12} + \frac{9}{12}$$
$$= 2\frac{9}{12} \text{ years}$$

Divide

Ann works 2,250 minutes in 5 days. How many minutes does she work each day?

$$2,250 \div 5 = 450 \text{ minutes}$$

For **1–9**, add, subtract, multiply, or divide.

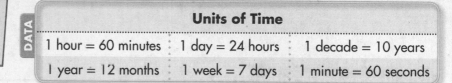

Units of Time

1 hour = 60 minutes	1 day = 24 hours	1 decade = 10 years
1 year = 12 months	1 week = 7 days	1 minute = 60 seconds

1. 8 hours 12 minutes
    + 3 hours 15 minutes

2. 9 weeks 5 days
    − 1 week 6 days

3. 3 hours 6 minutes 45 seconds
    + 8 hours 55 minutes 20 seconds

4. $3\frac{1}{12}$ years − $1\frac{9}{12}$ years

5. $2\frac{3}{4}$ months + $1\frac{2}{4}$ months

6. 245 days ÷ 5

7. What is 112 weeks ÷ 7?

8. What is $8 \times \frac{3}{4}$ hour?

9. How many years are in $\frac{2}{5}$ decade?

10. **Make Sense and Persevere** Beth works $8\frac{2}{4}$ hours, drives $1\frac{1}{4}$ hours, cooks $\frac{3}{4}$ hour, and sleeps $7\frac{2}{4}$ hours each day. How many hours of free time does Beth have each day? Remember, there are 24 hours in a day.

11. Ryan spends $10\frac{2}{4}$ hours at work each day. He has a $\frac{3}{4}$-hour lunch and receives two $\frac{1}{4}$-hour breaks. How much time does Ryan spend working?

12. The Baltimore Marathon features a relay race. The times for each leg run by a winning team are shown in the table at the right. What is the total time it took this team to run all four legs of the marathon?

Baltimore Marathon Winner Results	
Leg of Race	**Time Run**
Leg 1	32 minutes 56 seconds
Leg 2	42 minutes 28 seconds
Leg 3	34 minutes 34 seconds
Leg 4	39 minutes 2 seconds

DATA

13. **Use Appropriate Tools** What time does Mia have to leave for school if it takes 45 minutes to get to school? School starts at 7:30 A.M. Draw a number line to explain.

14. **Higher Order Thinking** Mr. Kent teaches 7 classes that are each $\frac{5}{6}$-hour long. He also has a $\frac{3}{6}$-hour lunch break. How much time does Mr. Kent spend teaching class and at lunch?

✓ **Assessment Practice**

15. Tom spends $\frac{2}{12}$ hour bathing a day. Megan spends $\frac{3}{12}$ hour a day bathing. How much more time does Megan spend bathing in 7 days than Tom?

16. Ari will be a teenager in $1\frac{3}{4}$ years. His little sister Anna will be one in $3\frac{1}{4}$ years. How much longer does Anna have to wait than Ari?

Name _____

Another Look!

How many more cups of bananas than cups of flour are in 3 loaves of banana bread?

Tell how you can model with math to solve problems.

- I can use previously learned concepts and skills.
- I can find and answer any hidden questions.
- I can use bar diagrams and equations to represent and solve this problem.

Draw bar diagrams and write equations to solve the hidden question and the original question.

Loaf of Banana Bread
$1\frac{3}{4}$ cups of mashed bananas
$1\frac{1}{4}$ cups flour
$\frac{1}{4}$ cup applesauce

When you model with math, you can write an equation to represent the relationships in the problem.

$1\frac{3}{4}$

$1\frac{1}{4}$	m

d

$\frac{2}{4}$	$\frac{2}{4}$	$\frac{2}{4}$

$1\frac{3}{4} - 1\frac{1}{4} = \frac{2}{4}$

Each loaf uses $\frac{2}{4}$ cup more of mashed bananas than flour.

$3 \times \frac{2}{4} = \frac{6}{4}$ or $1\frac{2}{4}$

3 loaves of banana bread contain $1\frac{2}{4}$ or $1\frac{1}{2}$ cups more mashed bananas than flour.

Model with Math

Aaron wraps presents in a store. In one hour, he wraps 8 games and one console. How much wrapping paper does Aaron use? Use Exercises 1–3 to answer the question.

1. Draw a bar diagram and write an equation to find g, how much paper Aaron uses on games.

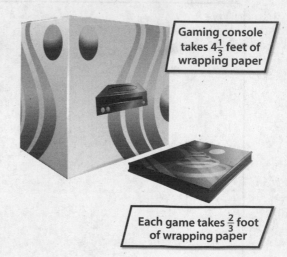

Gaming console takes $4\frac{1}{3}$ feet of wrapping paper

Each game takes $\frac{2}{3}$ foot of wrapping paper

2. Draw a bar diagram and write an equation to find t, the total amount of wrapping paper Aaron used.

3. What previously learned math did you use to solve the problem?

Cat Food

Tamara feeds her cat $\frac{1}{8}$ cup canned food each day and the rest dry. She also gives her cat one treat a day. How much dry food does Tamara feed her cat in a week?

4. **Reasoning** What quantities are given in the problem and what do the numbers describe?

$\frac{3}{8}$ cup of food per day

5. **Make Sense and Persevere** What do you need to find?

6. **Model with Math** Draw bar diagrams and write equations to find d, the amount of dry cat food Tamara feeds her cat each day and w, the amount in a week.

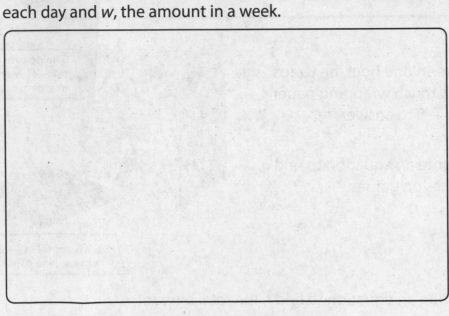

When you model with math, you use math to represent a problem situation.

7. **Be Precise** Explain how you know what units to use for your answer.

Practice Video Tools Games

Another Look!

The data table shows the distances Freda ran over a period of 17 days.

A line plot shows data along a number line. Each dot represents 1 day.

What is the difference between Freda's two longest runs?

Distance (miles)	Days
$\frac{1}{2}$	2
$1\frac{1}{2}$	4
2	5
$2\frac{1}{2}$	3
3	2
5	1

DATA

Freda's Daily Running Distance

0   $\frac{1}{2}$ 1 $1\frac{1}{2}$ 2 $2\frac{1}{2}$ 3 $3\frac{1}{2}$ 4 $4\frac{1}{2}$ 5

Miles

Freda's longest distance run is 5 miles. Her second longest distance run is 3 miles. The difference is 2 miles.

For **1–5**, use the line plot at the right.

1. How many puppies are at the pet store?

2. Which weight is the most common?

3. How many more puppies weighed 3 pounds than 7 pounds?

Use a fraction to name points on a number line that are not whole numbers.

4. How much more does the heaviest puppy weigh than the lightest?

Weights of Puppies at a Pet Store

3   4   5   6   7   8   9   10   11   12   13

Pounds

5. What is the total weight of all the puppies? Explain.

For **6–7**, use the line plot at the right.

6. Which height is the most common among the students in Ms. Jackson's class?

7. **Reasoning** What is the difference between the tallest height and the shortest height? Explain.

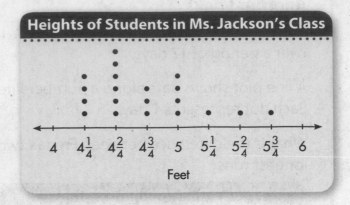

Heights of Students in Ms. Jackson's Class

Feet

For **8–9**, use the line plot at the right.

8. How many more plants are less than $3\frac{2}{4}$ inches than are greater than $3\frac{2}{4}$ inches? Explain.

9. **Higher Order Thinking** Write a question that can be answered by using the line plot, and then give the answer.

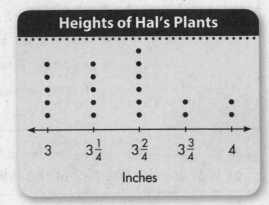

Heights of Hal's Plants

Inches

☑ **Assessment Practice**

For **10–11**, use the line plot at the right.

10. How many recipes use 2 cups of flour or more?

   Ⓐ 3 recipes

   Ⓑ 4 recipes

   Ⓒ 7 recipes

   Ⓓ 14 recipes

11. How much more flour goes into the recipe that uses the most than goes in the recipe that uses the least?

   Ⓐ $\frac{1}{4}$ cup   Ⓒ $1\frac{1}{4}$ cups

   Ⓑ $\frac{3}{4}$ cup   Ⓓ $1\frac{3}{4}$ cups

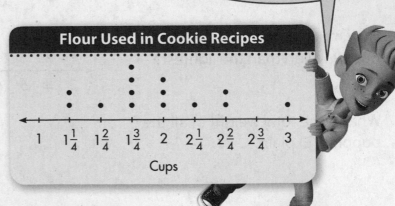

The number of recipes is represented by the number of dots on the line plot.

Flour Used in Cookie Recipes

Cups

Name _____

Another Look!

Dorothy measured the lengths of the fingers on her left hand. She also measured the length of her thumb. Dorothy wants to make a line plot to show the measurements.

Follow these steps to make a line plot.

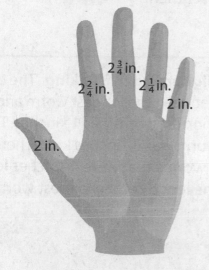

$2\frac{3}{4}$ in.
$2\frac{2}{4}$ in. $2\frac{1}{4}$ in.
2 in.
2 in.

Step 1

Draw a number line and choose a scale based on the data collected. The scale should show data values from least to greatest.

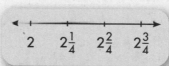

2    $2\frac{1}{4}$ $2\frac{2}{4}$ $2\frac{3}{4}$

Step 2

Write a title for the line plot and a label for the numbers.

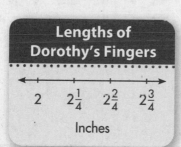

Lengths of Dorothy's Fingers

2    $2\frac{1}{4}$ $2\frac{2}{4}$ $2\frac{3}{4}$

Inches

Step 3

Draw a dot for each length.

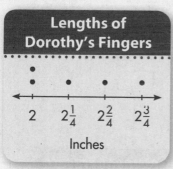

Lengths of Dorothy's Fingers

2    $2\frac{1}{4}$ $2\frac{2}{4}$ $2\frac{3}{4}$

Inches

For **1–4**, use the line plot at the right.

1. Aiden has two toy cars that measure $2\frac{2}{8}$ inches, three that measure $2\frac{3}{8}$ inches, one that measures $2\frac{7}{8}$ inches, one that measures $2\frac{1}{8}$ inches, and one that measures $2\frac{6}{8}$ inches. Use these data to complete the line plot at the right.

2. How long is Aiden's longest toy car?

3. If Aiden lined up his cars that are $2\frac{3}{8}$ inches long, how long would they all be?

4. Are more cars shorter or longer than $2\frac{4}{8}$ inches?

Lengths of Aiden's Cars

Inches

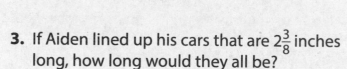

5. **Vocabulary** Use a vocabulary word to complete the sentence.

An _____ fraction names the same region, part of a set, or part of a segment.

6. enVision® STEM Floodwalls are used to prevent damage from floods. A town built a floodwall $4\frac{4}{8}$ feet tall. Another town built a floodwall $7\frac{1}{8}$ feet tall. What is the difference between the heights of the floodwalls?

7. Higher Order Thinking The difference between the longest worm and the shortest worm was $1\frac{2}{4}$ inches. The shortest worm was $3\frac{1}{4}$ inches long. There were 2 worms that were $4\frac{1}{4}$ inches long. Find the length of the longest worm.

8. Tony wants to make a line plot of the distances he rode his bike last week. He rode the following distances in miles:

$3, 4\frac{1}{2}, 6, 3, 5\frac{1}{2}, 3, 5\frac{1}{2}$

Make a line plot for the distances Tony rode.

✓ Assessment Practice

9. Caden collects insects. The table below lists the lengths in inches of insects in Caden's collection.

Insect	Length (in.)
Ladybug	$\frac{2}{8}$
Cross Spider	$\frac{6}{8}$
Honey Bee	$\frac{4}{8}$
Field Cricket	$\frac{6}{8}$
Big Dipper Firefly	$\frac{4}{8}$
Stag Beetle	1

Use the data set to complete the line plot.

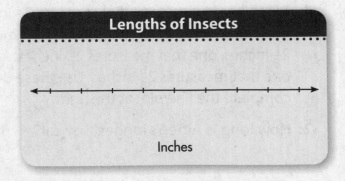

Lengths of Insects

Inches

Another Look!

Ryan's dog just had a litter of 8 puppies. He measured the length of each of the puppies. The line plot below shows their lengths in inches. Ryan says the longest puppy in the litter is $7\frac{4}{8}$ inches because $7\frac{4}{8}$ has the most dots above it.

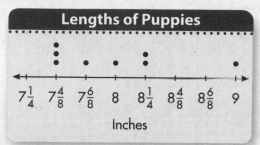

Tell how you can critique Ryan's reasoning.

Ryan's reasoning does not make sense. The most dots shows the most common length of puppy. To find the longest puppy, Ryan should find the dot farthest to the right on the line plot.

The longest puppy in the litter is 9 inches.

When you critique reasoning, you explain why someone's reasoning is correct or incorrect.

Critique Reasoning

Sandy made this line plot to show how many hours she read on each of 10 days. She said the difference between the greatest time and the least time she read in one day was $1\frac{3}{4}$ hours.

1. Tell how you can critique Sandy's reasoning.

2. Critique Sandy's reasoning.

Critique Reasoning

Liana has a collection of books in her library. The line plot below shows the lengths of her books. Liana says that her longest book is 6 inches in length.

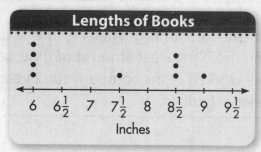

3. Tell how you can critique Liana's reasoning.

4. Critique Liana's reasoning.

Math Is Fun

Nine employees work at Math Is Fun Co. The table lists the number of years each employee has worked at the company.

Employee	Employed at Math Is Fun Co. (Years)
1	2
2	$3\frac{2}{4}$
3	$1\frac{2}{4}$
4	$2\frac{3}{4}$
5	5
6	$1\frac{2}{4}$
7	$4\frac{2}{4}$
8	$5\frac{1}{4}$
9	2

5. **Model with Math** Draw a line plot to show the number of years 9 employees have worked at Math Is Fun Co. Explain why a line plot can make it easier to find the most common number of years people worked at the company.

6. **Critique Reasoning** Wallace, one of the employees who has been there the least amount of time, says in $\frac{3}{4}$ of a year, he will have worked at the company for 2 years. Do you agree with Wallace? Explain.

When you critique reasoning, you consider all parts of an argument.

7. **Make Sense and Persevere** Which employee has been at Math Is Fun Co. for the longest time? How much longer has that employee been working than the employee who has been there the shortest amount of time? Explain.

Name _____

Another Look!

How can you represent a number as a fraction or a decimal?

30 parts out of 100 is 0.30.

$$\frac{30}{100} = 0.30$$

3 parts out of 10 is 0.3.

$$\frac{3}{10} = 0.3$$

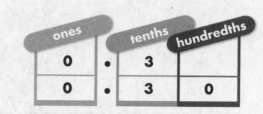

ones		tenths	hundredths
0	.	3	
0	.	3	0

So, $\frac{30}{100} = \frac{3}{10}$ and 0.30 = 0.3. These decimals and fractions are equivalent.

For **1–3**, write a decimal and fraction for each grid.

1.

2.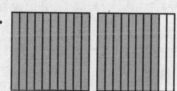

3.

For **4–7**, shade the grid for each fraction and write the decimal.

4. $\frac{1}{10}$

5. $\frac{8}{10}$

6. $\frac{29}{100}$

7. $\frac{4}{100}$

8. On Tuesday, Pierce ran $\frac{3}{4}$ mile and walked $\frac{3}{4}$ mile. On Wednesday, he ran $\frac{2}{4}$ mile and walked $1\frac{1}{4}$ miles. How much farther did Pierce run and walk on Wednesday than on Tuesday? Explain.

9. Critique Reasoning Monique said, "0.70 is greater than 0.7 because 70 is greater than 7." Do you agree with Monique? Why or why not?

10. Write the value of the shaded parts of the grids to the right 4 different ways.

11. Jaclynn had 84 cents. Her brother gave her another 61 cents. Write the amount of money Jaclynn now has as a decimal. Explain.

12. Higher Order Thinking Hugh uses 0.63 of a piece of canvas to paint a picture. Draw a model to represent this decimal. How much of the canvas is left?

Assessment Practice

13. Select all that are equivalent to the part of the grid that is shaded.

☐ $\frac{7}{10}$

☐ $\frac{7}{100}$

☐ 0.7

☐ 0.07

☐ 0.70

14. Which fraction and decimal represent the shaded part of the grid below?

Ⓐ $8\frac{5}{10}$; 8.5

Ⓑ $\frac{85}{100}$; 0.85

Ⓒ $\frac{15}{100}$; 0.15

Ⓓ $\frac{85}{10}$; 0.85

Name _____

Another Look!

Patrick collected change for charity. On Friday, he collected $7.28. On Saturday, he collected $7.15. On which day did Patrick collect more money? Use a number line to compare the amounts.

```
            $7.15        $7.28
   ←+++++++++|++++++•++++++•++++++++|+++++++→
   $7.00   $7.10   $7.20   $7.30   $7.40   $7.50
```

Because $7.28 is farther to the right on the number line, it is the greater number.

So, $7.28 > $7.15.

Patrick collected more money on Friday.

You can use different tools including number lines, grids, or place-value blocks to help you compare decimals. When using place-value blocks, let the flat equal one whole.

For **1–11**, write >, <, or = in each ◯. Use an appropriate tool as needed to compare.

1.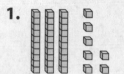

0.37 ◯ 0.77

2.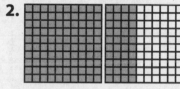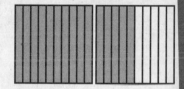

1.40 ◯ 1.5

3. 0.6 ◯ 0.55

4. 0.2 ◯ 0.20

5. 0.68 ◯ 0.59

6. $10.45 ◯ $10.54

7. 0.99 ◯ 1.0

8. 0.05 ◯ 0.04

9. 4.1 ◯ 4.10

10. 6.44 ◯ 6.4

11. $0.93 ◯ $0.39

For **12–20**, write a decimal to make each comparison true.

12. _____ > 1.45

13. 7.8 = _____

14. _____ > 4.42

15. 29.20 > _____

16. 8.99 < _____

17. 13.40 = _____

18. 22.18 < _____

19. _____ > 3.48

20. 9.4 > _____

21. Mark told Patrick that his quarter weighs less than what a nickel weighs because 0.2 has fewer digits than 0.18. How can Patrick show Mark that 0.2 is greater than 0.18?

Quarter 0.2 oz

Nickel 0.18 oz

22. Critique Reasoning Kimmy drew the number line below and wrote the comparison shown. Is her comparison correct? Explain.

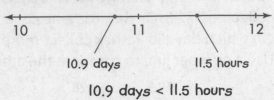

10.9 days < 11.5 hours

23. 🔤 **Vocabulary** Use a vocabulary term to make the sentence true.

In 37.2, the ones place and the tenths place are separated by a _____.

24. Higher Order Thinking Tamar is thinking of a number in the hundredths. Her number is greater than 0.8 and less than 0.9. The greatest digit in the number is in the hundredths place. What number is Tamar thinking of? Explain.

☑ **Assessment Practice**

25. Andy mailed two packages. The first package weighed 2.48 pounds, and the second weighed 2.6 pounds. Andy said, "The first package will cost more to send because it weighs more."

Part A

How can you convince Andy that the second package weighs more?

Part B

Andy mailed a third package weighing 2.5 pounds. Did the third package weigh more or less than the first package? Describe how you would use place-value blocks to compare the weights.

Practice Video Tools Games

Another Look!

In the morning, Duncan sold $\frac{27}{100}$ of the items in his yard sale. In the afternoon, he sold another $\frac{6}{10}$ of the items.

What fraction of the items did Duncan sell?

Find $\frac{27}{100} + \frac{6}{10}$.

Use equivalent fractions to find how many of the items Duncan sold.

Rename one of the fractions to have a common denominator.

$$\frac{6 \times 10}{10 \times 10} = \frac{60}{100}$$

Add

$$\frac{27}{100} + \frac{60}{100} = \frac{87}{100}$$

Duncan sold $\frac{87}{100}$ of the items.

For **1–15**, add the fractions.

1. $\frac{31}{100} + \frac{4}{10} = \frac{31}{100} + \frac{\square}{100} = \frac{\square}{100}$

2. $\frac{17}{100} + \frac{9}{10} = \frac{17}{100} + \frac{\square}{\square} = 1\frac{7}{100}$

3. $\frac{\square}{100} + \frac{3}{\square} = \frac{2}{\square} + \frac{\square}{10} = \frac{5}{10}$

4. $\frac{6}{10} + \frac{39}{100}$

5. $\frac{7}{10} + \frac{22}{100}$

6. $\frac{9}{100} + \frac{3}{10} + \frac{5}{10}$

7. $2\frac{4}{10} + \frac{33}{100}$

8. $\frac{19}{100} + \frac{21}{100} + \frac{3}{10}$

9. $\frac{9}{10} + \frac{30}{100}$

10. $\frac{1}{100} + \frac{25}{10}$

11. $1\frac{3}{10} + 2\frac{8}{100}$

12. $\frac{27}{100} + \frac{2}{10}$

13. $\frac{3}{10} + \frac{4}{10} + \frac{53}{100}$

14. $\frac{64}{100} + \frac{33}{100}$

15. $3\frac{3}{10} + \frac{42}{100} + \frac{33}{100}$

16. Model with Math Cecily purchases a box of 100 paper clips. She puts $\frac{37}{100}$ of the paper clips in a jar on her desk and puts another $\frac{6}{10}$ in her drawer at home. Shade a grid that shows how many of the paper clips are in Cecily's jar and drawer, then write the fraction the grid represents.

17. Robyn sells 100 tickets to the fourth-grade play. The table shows the part of the tickets she sold of each type. What fraction of the tickets were adult and student tickets?

Ticket	Number
Adult	$\frac{38}{100}$
Child	$\frac{22}{100}$
Student	$\frac{4}{10}$

DATA

18. enVision® STEM Balls colliding on a pool table are an example of how energy transfers when objects collide. When two balls collide, the first ball loses speed and the second ball moves. What is the combined distance the two balls traveled?

$\frac{5}{10}$ m $\frac{33}{100}$ m

19. Higher Order Thinking Alecia walked $\frac{3}{10}$ of a mile from school, stopped at the grocery store on the way, then walked another $\frac{4}{10}$ of a mile home. Georgia walked $\frac{67}{100}$ of a mile from school to her home. Which of the girls walked farther home from school? Explain.

✓ **Assessment Practice**

20. Regina kept a reading log of how much of her 100-page book she read each day. She read $\frac{33}{100}$ of the book on Monday, $\frac{4}{10}$ of the book on Tuesday, and another $\frac{35}{100}$ of the book on Wednesday. Did Regina fill out her reading log correctly? Explain.

Use what you know about fractions to solve.

 Practice Video Tools Games

Another Look!

Add

$1.25 + $2.01

$1.25 + $2.01 = $3.26

Subtract

$2.28 − $1.25

$2.28 − $1.25 = $1.03

> You can use coins and bills to add, subtract, multiply, and divide with money.

Multiply

2 × $2.01

2 × $2.01 = $4.02

Divide

$3.03 ÷ 3

$3.03 ÷ 3 = $1.01

For **1–2**, draw or use coins and bills to solve.

1. Mrs. Hargrove owes the doctor $34.56. She gives the clerk $50.00.

   a. List Mrs. Hargrove's change using the least number of coins and bills.

   b. What is the total amount of change Mrs. Hargrove should receive?

2. Emma buys a game for $26.84. She gives the clerk $30.00.

   a. List Emma's change using the least number of coins and bills.

   b. What is the total amount of change Emma should receive?

3. Model with Math Three friends combine their money to buy tickets for a hockey game. If they share the change evenly, how much will each friend receive? Write equations to represent the problem, then solve.

Money given for tickets

---

4. Niall has a half dollar, Krista has a quarter dollar, Mary has a tenth of a dollar, and Jack has a hundredth of a dollar. If they combine their money, do the 4 students have more or less than a dollar? Explain.

5. Jessie has 14 half-dollar coins, but she needs quarters to do her laundry. If she trades her half-dollar coins for quarters, how many quarters will Jessie have? Explain.

---

6. Higher Order Thinking Julia and Carl buy 2 sandwiches, 1 salad, 1 piece of fruit, and 2 drinks for lunch. They give the cashier $20.03. What coins and bills could they receive in change? Draw or use coins and bills to solve.

Menu	
Sandwich	$3.96
Chips	$0.79
Fruit	$1.24
Salad	$2.17
Drink	$1.55

✓ **Assessment Practice**

7. Claire has a $60 gift card. She uses the whole value of the card to buy 4 copies of the same book to give as gifts. How much does each book cost?

Ⓐ $15

Ⓑ $20

Ⓒ $40

Ⓓ $60

8. Larisa buys 3 purses. Each purse costs $126.32. How much did Larisa spend? Draw or use bills and coins to solve.

Ⓐ $126.32

Ⓑ $256.64

Ⓒ $378.96

Ⓓ $505.28

Additional Practice 12-6
Look For and Use Structure

Another Look!

Do the number lines show 0.2 = 0.5?

Tell how you can use the structure of a number line to analyze the relationships between decimals.

- I can break the problem into simpler parts.

- I can use what I know about decimal meanings.

Use the number line to help you find if the decimals represent parts of the same whole.

On the third number line, you can use the distance between 0 and 0.2 as a guide to mark **0.4, 0.6, 0.8,** and **1**.

On the fourth number line, you can use the distance between 0 and 0.5 as a guide to mark **1**.

When the size of the whole is not the same on the two number lines, the number lines cannot be used to show equivalent decimals.

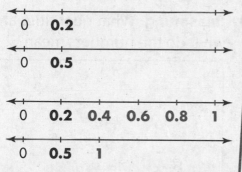

Use Structure

Anton knows it is $\frac{1}{2}$ mile from his home to the store along Main Street. He wants to find how far it is from his home to school.

Home   Store   School

1. Label 1, 1.5, and 2 on the drawing. Explain how you determined where to label each number.

> When you look for relationships, you use equivalent forms of numbers.

2. How far does Anton live from school? Explain.

Training

Liz trains for rock climbing 4 days a week. Her first 4 days of training are shown in the table. She plans to increase the distance each time she climbs. Did Liz climb farther on the first two days than the last two days?

DATA	Day	Distance Liz Climbed
	1	0.09 km
	2	0.1 km
	3	0.11 km
	4	0.07 km

3. **Reasoning** What quantities are given in the problem and what do the numbers mean?

4. **Make Sense and Persevere** What do you need to find?

5. **Make Sense and Persevere** What hidden questions need to be answered before answering the main question?

When you look for relationships, you break problems into simpler parts to solve.

6. **Model with Math** Use equivalent fractions to write equations to find the distances Liz climbed the first two days and the last two days.

7. **Construct Arguments** Did Liz climb farther the first two days or the last two days? Use a number line to justify your answer.

Name _____

Another Look!

Joe's cat, Tiger, is $2\frac{1}{6}$ feet long. Casey's cat, Fluffy, is $\frac{3}{6}$ yard long. Which cat is longer? How much longer?

Be precise and use the correct units.

Step 1

Change Fluffy's length to feet and compare.

$$\frac{3}{6} \times 3 = \frac{3 \times 3}{6}$$

$$= \frac{9}{6} = \frac{6}{6} + \frac{3}{6} = 1\frac{3}{6}$$

Fluffy is $1\frac{3}{6}$ feet long.

Compare the lengths.

$$2\frac{1}{6} > 1\frac{3}{6}$$

Tiger is longer.

Step 2

Find the difference. Use a linear model to help.

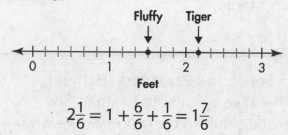

$$2\frac{1}{6} = 1 + \frac{6}{6} + \frac{1}{6} = 1\frac{7}{6}$$

$$2\frac{1}{6} - 1\frac{3}{6} = 1\frac{7}{6} - 1\frac{3}{6} = \frac{4}{6}$$

Tiger is $\frac{4}{6}$ foot longer than Fluffy.

In **1–3**, write > or < in each ⭕ to compare the measures.

1. 8 inches ⭕ 8 feet   **2.** 5 yards ⭕ 12 feet   **3.** 3 yards ⭕ 90 inches

For **4–7**, convert each unit.

4. 25 feet = _____ inches   **5.** 3 miles = _____ feet

6. $\frac{1}{2}$ yard = _____ inches   **7.** 57 yards = _____ inches

For **8–9**, complete each table.

8.

Feet	Inches
2	
4	
6	
8	

9.

Yards	Inches
1	
2	
3	
4	

For **10–12**, use the picture at the right.

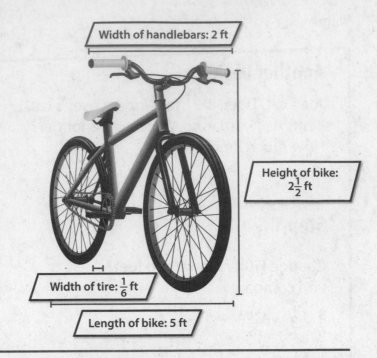

Width of handlebars: 2 ft

Height of bike: $2\frac{1}{2}$ ft

Width of tire: $\frac{1}{6}$ ft

Length of bike: 5 ft

10. Be Precise How many more feet is the length of the bike than the height of the bike?

11. What is the width of the tire in inches?

12. Each handle is $\frac{1}{4}$ the width of the handlebars. How many inches long is each handle?

---

13. Make Sense and Persevere Harriet rode her bike $2\frac{1}{4}$ miles to the mall. She then rode $\frac{3}{4}$ mile to the grocery store. She came back the way she went. How many miles did Harriet ride in all? Explain.

14. Higher Order Thinking Use the linear model. What fraction of 1 foot is 3 inches? What fraction of 1 yard is 3 inches? Explain.

```
0   3   6   9  12 in.              1 yd
            1 ft        2 ft       3 ft
```

✅ **Assessment Practice**

15. Vulkan jumped $\frac{7}{8}$ yard and then $2\frac{7}{8}$ feet. How many feet did he jump in all? Show both measures with points on the number line.

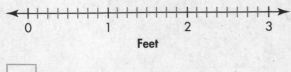

Feet

☐ feet

16. A medium sandwich at Heidi's Heros is $\frac{5}{8}$ foot long. A small sandwich is $4\frac{7}{8}$ inches. How many inches longer is the medium than the small?

Ⓐ $2\frac{5}{8}$ inches

Ⓑ $2\frac{7}{8}$ inches

Ⓒ $3\frac{3}{8}$ inches

Ⓓ $4\frac{2}{8}$ inches

Another Look!

Lance has an 8-gallon aquarium. How many 2-quart containers will it take to fill the aquarium?

Customary Units of Capacity

DATA

1 cup (c) = 8 fluid ounces (fl oz)

1 pint (pt) = 2 c = 16 fl oz

1 quart (qt) = 2 pt = 4 c

1 gallon (gal) = 4 qt = 8 pt

Step 1

Convert 8 gallons to quarts.

Gallons	Quarts
2	8
4	16
6	24
8	32

8 gallons = 32 quarts

Use the correct units as you solve measurement problems.

Step 2

Divide 32 quarts by 2.

$$\begin{array}{r} 16 \\ 2\overline{)32} \\ -2 \\ \hline 12 \\ -12 \\ \hline 0 \end{array}$$

It takes 16 of the 2-quart containers to fill the aquarium.

In **1–3**, write > or < in each ◯ to compare the measures.

1. 5 quarts ◯ 5 cups

2. 5 cups ◯ 3 pints

3. 18 pints ◯ 2 gallons

For **4–7**, convert each unit.

4. 3 pints = _____ fluid ounces

5. 16 quarts = _____ cups

6. 2 gallons = _____ pints

7. $\frac{1}{2}$ gallon = _____ fluid ounces

For **8–9**, complete each table.

8.

Quarts	Pints
1	
2	
3	
4	

9.

Gallons	Pints
$\frac{1}{2}$	
1	
2	
3	

10. **Make Sense and Persevere** Edgar has a birdbath that holds 3 quarts of water. He only wants to fill it $\frac{3}{4}$ full. How many 1-pint containers does it take to fill the birdbath? How could he fill it with pint and cup containers? Explain.

11. How many minutes are in 3 hours? There are 60 minutes in one hour. Complete the table.

Hours	Minutes
1	
2	
3	

12. **enVision® STEM** How many pounds of eroded material does the Verde River carry past a given point in $\frac{1}{4}$ of a day? There are 24 hours in a day. Explain.

The Verde River in Arizona carries an average of 860 pounds of eroded material past a given point each hour.

13. A car with a 20-gallon gas tank can go 25 miles on 1 gallon of gas. If the tank is full at the beginning of a 725-mile trip, how many times does the driver have to refill the gas tank?

14. **Higher Order Thinking** Janice needs 3 gallons of lemonade for a party. She has 4 quarts, 6 pints, and 4 cups of lemonade already made. How many more cups of lemonade does Janice need?

✓ **Assessment Practice**

15. Which equals 6 pints?

Ⓐ 6 cups

Ⓑ 24 cups

Ⓒ 2 gallons

Ⓓ 3 quarts

16. Select all the comparisons that are true.

☐ 4 cups $<$ 40 fluid ounces

☐ 9 pints $>$ 9 quarts

☐ 3 gallons $<$ 16 quarts

☐ 5 quarts $<$ 24 cups

☐ 2 gallons $<$ 20 cups

Name _____

Another Look!

The world's largest horse weighed almost 3,000 pounds. An average mature male horse weighs about $\frac{3}{5}$ ton. How much more did the largest horse weigh than an average horse?

Step 1

Convert the weight of the average horse to pounds. Use the model.

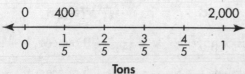

Pounds

0   400   2,000

0    $\frac{1}{5}$ $\frac{2}{5}$ $\frac{3}{5}$ $\frac{4}{5}$ 1

Tons

$\frac{3}{5}$ tons = 1,200 pounds

Step 2

Find the difference.

3,000 lb	
1,200 lb	d

$d = 3,000 - 1,200$
$d = 1,800$

The world's largest horse weighed 1,800 pounds more than an average male horse.

There are 2,000 pounds in a ton.

In **1–3**, write > or < in each ◯ to compare the measures.

1. 8 ounces ◯ 8 pounds

2. 75 ounces ◯ 5 pounds

3. 7,000 pounds ◯ 3 tons

For **4–7**, convert each unit.

4. 21 pounds = _____ ounces

5. 8 tons = _____ pounds

6. 6 tons = _____ pounds

7. $\frac{1}{2}$ pound = _____ ounces

For **8–9**, complete each table.

8.

Tons	Pounds
1	2,000
2	
3	

9.

Pounds	Ounces
1	16
2	
3	

For **10–12**, use the table and art shown at the right.

10. **Be Precise** What is the total weight in ounces of Heidi's two guinea pigs?

11. **Be Precise** What is the total weight in ounces of the food for Heidi's guinea pigs?

Heidi's two guinea pigs each weigh $2\frac{1}{2}$ pounds.

12. **Higher Order Thinking** A pound of guinea-pig pellets is about 3 cups of food. Each guinea pig eats $\frac{1}{4}$ cup of pellets a day. How many days will the pellets last? Explain.

Food for Heidi's Guinea Pigs	
Food	**Weight**
Grass or hay	40 ounces
Vegetables	15 ounces
Pellets	5 pounds

DATA

13. **Number Sense** Which product is greater, 9×15 or 9×17? Explain how you can tell without finding the products.

14. Which is greater, $\frac{1}{12}$ pound or 2 ounces? Explain.

Assessment Practice

15. Which is most likely to weigh 4 tons?
  Ⓐ A cherry
  Ⓑ A man
  Ⓒ A bag of potatoes
  Ⓓ A helicopter

16. Which comparison is true?
  Ⓐ 5,000 pounds $<$ 2 tons
  Ⓑ 6 pounds $>$ 98 ounces
  Ⓒ 36 ounces $<$ 2 pounds
  Ⓓ 4 pounds $>$ 60 ounces

Name _____

Another Look!

Jasmine finished 9 centimeters of the scarf she is knitting. Manuella finished 108 millimeters of her scarf. How much longer is Manuella's scarf than Jasmine's?

To change from a larger unit like centimeters to a smaller unit like millimeters, multiply.

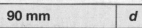

Step 1

Convert 9 centimeters to millimeters.

1 centimeter = 10 millimeters

$9 \times 10 = 90$ millimeters

Number of centimeters — Millimeters per centimeter

9 centimeters = 90 millimeters

Step 2

Find the difference, d.

108 mm	
90 mm	d

$108 - 90 = d$

$d = 18$

Manuella's scarf is 18 millimeters longer than Jasmine's scarf.

In **1–3**, tell what metric unit you would use to measure each.

1. Height of a tree

2. The width of a kernel of corn

3. The length of your arm

For **4–7**, convert each unit.

4. 7 meters = _____ centimeters

5. 8 kilometers = _____ meters

6. 65 centimeters = _____ millimeters

7. 2 meters = _____ centimeters

For **8–9**, complete each table.

8.

Kilometers	Meters
1	1,000
2	
3	

9.

Meters	Centimeters
1	100
2	
3	

10. Brittney bought two bottles of shampoo like the one shown and paid $0.52 tax. How much did she spend? Use bills and coins to solve.

11. Brittney paid for the shampoo with a $20 bill. How much change did Brittney get back? Use bills and coins to solve.

$2.88

DAILY
MOISTURE
SHAMPOO

For All Hair
23.7 FL OZ.

12. Jason is 1.4 meters tall. His brother is 0.9 meter tall. Who is taller? Show each height on the linear model. Explain.

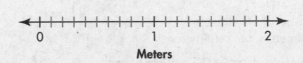

Meters

13. Martha had 2.35 centimeters of her hair cut off. Neil had 2.53 centimeters cut. Who had more hair cut off? Explain.

14. A spider traveled 3 meters in one minute. How many centimeters did it travel?

15. **Be Precise** The ceiling of Mr. Vega's classroom is 3 meters high. The ceiling in the hall is 315 centimeters high. How much taller is the ceiling in the hall than in the classroom?

16. **Higher Order Thinking** A yellow ribbon is 56 centimeters long. It is twice as long as a green ribbon. A brown ribbon is 4 times as long as the green ribbon. What is the length of the brown ribbon?

☑ **Assessment Practice**

17. Select all the true statements.

☐ 1,000 kilometers = 100 meters

☐ 11 meters = 110 centimeters

☐ 17 centimeters = 170 millimeters

☐ 5 meters = 500 millimeters

☐ 5 kilometers = 5,000 meters

18. Select all the true comparisons.

☐ 5 meters $>$ 200 millimeters

☐ 18 kilometers $<$ 1,800 meters

☐ 21 centimeters $>$ 200 millimeters

☐ 7 meters $<$ 70 centimeters

☐ 6 meters $>$ 6,200 millimeters

Another Look!

Convert each unit.

To convert from kilograms to grams, multiply by 1,000.

To convert from liters to milliliters, multiply by 1,000.

Convert 8 liters to milliliters.

1 liter = 1,000 milliliters

$8 \times 1,000 = 8,000$

8 liters = 8,000 milliliters

Convert 9 grams to milligrams.

1 gram = 1,000 milligrams

$9 \times 1,000 = 9,000$

9 grams = 9,000 milligrams

In **1–3**, tell what metric unit you would use to measure each.

1. Water in a washing machine

2. The mass of a large dog

3. The mass of a grape

For **4–7**, convert each unit.

4. 2 liters = _____ milliliters

5. 8 grams = _____ milligrams

6. 3 kilograms = _____ grams

7. 7 liters = _____ milliliters

For **8–9**, complete each table.

8.

Liters	Milliliters
7	
8	
9	

9.

Kilograms	Grams
4	
5	
6	

10. A-Z **Vocabulary** Fill in the blank: _____ is the amount of matter something contains. _____ is a measure of how heavy an object is.

11. Would a cup hold 250 liters of liquid or 250 milliliters of liquid? Explain.

12. enVision® STEM A glacier moved a boulder with a mass of 9 kilograms. What was the mass of the boulder in grams?

Glaciers move boulders, and boulders erode the soil.

13. Another glacier moved a boulder that weighed 2 tons. How many pounds did the boulder weigh?

14. **Reasoning** Hannah has 3 boxes of rice. One box contains 3 kilograms, the second box contains 150 grams, and the third box contains 500 grams. She wants to divide the rice equally into 5 bags. How much rice should she put into each bag? Explain.

15. **Higher Order Thinking** Rob has a 2-liter bottle of iced tea. He poured an equal amount of the iced tea into 8 containers. How many milliliters did Rob pour into each container?

☑ **Assessment Practice**

16. Which shows a correct comparison?

Ⓐ 1,000 liters < 1,000 milliliters

Ⓑ 40 liters < 400 milliliters

Ⓒ 5,100 milliliters > 5 liters

Ⓓ 900 milliliters > 900 liters

17. Which statement is true?

Ⓐ 5 grams = 500 milligrams

Ⓑ 1 gram = 10 milligrams

Ⓒ 910 kilograms = 910 grams

Ⓓ 2 kilograms = 2,000 grams

Practico   Video   Tools   Games

Another Look!

Find the perimeter of the rectangle.

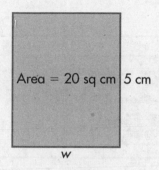

Area = 20 sq cm   5 cm

w

The length and width of a rectangle are used to find both the perimeter and the area of the figure.

Use the formula for the area of a rectangle to find the width.

$A = \ell \times w$

$20 = 5 \times w$

$w = 4$

The width of the rectangle is 4 centimeters.

Use the formula for perimeter to find the perimeter of the rectangle.

$P = (2 \times \ell) + (2 \times w)$

$P = (2 \times 5) + (2 \times 4)$

$P = 10 + 8 = 18$

The perimeter of the rectangle is 18 centimeters.

For **1–4**, use the formulas for perimeter and area to solve each problem.

1. Find n.

2 ft   Area = 28 sq ft

$\overset{\longmapsto n \longmapsto}{}$

2. Find n. Then find the area.
Perimeter = 86 in.

25 in.

n

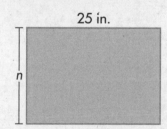

3. Find n. Then find the perimeter.

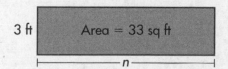

3 ft   Area = 33 sq ft

n

4. Find n. Perimeter = $60\frac{2}{4}$ in.

$\overset{\longmapsto n \longmapsto}{}$

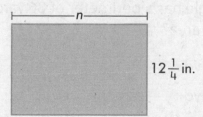

$12\frac{1}{4}$ in.

5. On Friday, 39,212 fans attended the baseball game at a major league baseball park. On Saturday, 41,681 fans attended, and on Sunday 42,905 fans attended. How many more fans attended on Saturday and Sunday than on Friday?

6. What is the area of a square with a perimeter of 28 feet?

7. One side of the flower garden is 3 times as long as the other. What are the dimensions of the flower garden?

Area = 48 sq m

8. The sides of each square in the potholder measure 1 inch. What are the perimeter and area of the potholder?

9. How many seconds are in 3 minutes? There are 60 seconds in one minute. Complete the table.

Minutes	Seconds
1	
2	
3	

10. Higher Order Thinking An art class is planning to paint a rectangular mural with an area of 60 square feet. It has to be at least 4 feet high but no more than 6 feet high. The length and width have to be whole numbers. List all possible widths for the mural.

11. The rectangle has a perimeter of 86 yards. Which is its area?

15 yd

Ⓐ 210 sq yd

Ⓑ 420 sq yd

Ⓒ 560 sq yd

Ⓓ 840 sq yd

Practice Video Tools Games

Another Look!

Mia has a length of string that is 2 meters long. She cuts it into 4 equal pieces. Is one of the pieces of string long enough to tie around the perimeter of a square box with a side length of 16 centimeters? Explain.

Tell how you can solve the problem with accuracy.

When you are precise, you use math symbols and language appropriately.

- I can correctly use the information given.

- I can calculate accurately.

- I can decide if my answer is clear and appropriate.

- I can use the correct units.

Attend to precision as you solve.

First, convert 2 meters to centimeters. $2 \times 100 = 200$ centimeters

Next, find the length of each piece Mia has after she cuts the string into 4 equal pieces. $200 \div 4 = 50$ centimeters

Then, find the perimeter of the square box. $P = 4 \times 16 = 64$ centimeters

The 50-centimeter piece is not long enough to go around the 64-centimeter perimeter of the box.

Be Precise

Susan bought a 1 kilogram bag of grapes. On the way home, she ate 125 grams of the grapes. How many grams of grapes does Susan have left? Use Exercises 1–3 to solve.

1. How can you use the information given to solve the problem?

2. How many grams of grapes does Susan have left? Show that you computed accurately.

3. Use math language and symbols to explain how you used the correct measurement units to solve the problem.

Cell Phone Pouches

Lex wants to make phone bags like the one shown. The pattern shows the material he needs for each side of the bag. He needs to know how much material he will need to make each bag.

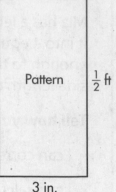

Pattern $\frac{1}{2}$ ft

3 in.

7 ½ inches of string

4. **Make Sense and Persevere** What do you know, and what do you need to find?

5. **Model with Math** Write and solve equations to explain how to solve. Tell what your variables mean.

When you are precise, you give carefully formulated explanations that are clear and appropriate.

6. **Be Precise** Explain how you know what units to use for your answer.

7. **Reasoning** What information was not needed to solve the problem?

Name _____

Another Look!

Melanie is creating a pattern using the rule "Add 11." Her starting number is 11. What are the next 5 numbers in Melanie's pattern? Describe a feature of the pattern.

You can use a rule to describe a number pattern.

Use the rule to continue the pattern.

+11 +11 +11 +11 +11
11   22   33   44   55   66

The next 5 numbers in Melanie's pattern are 22, 33, 44, 55, and 66.

Describe features of the pattern.

- The numbers in the pattern are multiples of 11.

- The digits in the ones place increase by one as the pattern continues.

For **1–6**, continue each pattern. Describe a feature of each pattern.

1. Subtract 2: 30, 28, 26, _____, _____

2. Add 8: 14, 22, 30, _____, _____

3. Add 9: 108, 117, 126, _____, _____

4. Subtract 7: 161, 154, 147, _____, _____

5. Add 10: 213, 223, 233, _____, _____

6. Subtract 18: 452, 434, 416, _____, _____

For **7–12**, use the rule to fill in the missing number in each pattern.

7. Add 3

41, 44, _____, 50

8. Subtract 10

429, 419, 409, _____

9. Add 16

27, _____, 59, 75

10. Add 11

117, _____, 139, 150

11. Subtract 2, Add 3

6, 4, 7, _____, _____

12. Add 2, Subtract 4

10, 12, 8, _____, _____

13. **Make Sense and Persevere** Emily buys a sandwich, a salad, and a drink. If she gives the cashier $20, how much change will she receive? Use bills and coins to solve.

DATA	Item	Price
	Sandwich	$5.75
	Salad	$3.25
	Drink	$1.45

14. Mimi started a pattern with 55 and used the rule "Add 10." What are the first five numbers in Mimi's pattern? Describe a feature of the pattern.

15. Jack arranged the pencils in groups of 6 to make a pattern. His rule is "Add 6." His starting number is 6. What are the next 4 numbers in Jack's pattern?

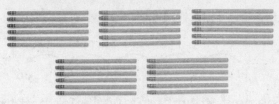

16. Presidential elections are held every 4 years. There were Presidential elections in 1840, 1844, 1848, and 1852. When were the next three Presidential elections? Describe a feature of the pattern.

17. **Higher Order Thinking** Sarah created a pattern. Her rule was "Add 4." All the numbers in Sarah's pattern were odd. Three of the numbers in Sarah's pattern were less than 10. What was the starting number for Sarah's pattern?

✓ **Assessment Practice**

18. The house numbers on Carr Memorial Avenue follow a pattern. The first four houses on the left side of the street are numbered 1408, 1414, 1420, and 1426. The rule is "Add 6." How many more houses are on the left side of the street with numbers less than 1450?

Ⓐ 1 house

Ⓑ 2 houses

Ⓒ 3 houses

Ⓓ 4 houses

19. Noreen is training for a race. The first week, she runs the route in 54 minutes. The second week, she runs the route in 52 minutes. The third week, she runs the route in 50 minutes. Noreen runs 2 minutes faster each week. If the pattern continues, how many minutes will it take Noreen to run the route the fifth week?

Ⓐ 44 minutes

Ⓑ 46 minutes

Ⓒ 48 minutes

Ⓓ 50 minutes

Name _____

Another Look!

Stephanie wants to know how many players are participating in a competition. There are 6 teams. Each team has 11 players. The rule is "Multiply by 11."

Use the rule to complete the table.

Number of Teams	Number of Players
1	11
2	22
3	33
4	44
5	55
6	66

Describe features of the pattern.

- The number of players are multiples of 11.

- The digits in the ones place increase by 1 for each team added.

- The number of teams is a factor of the number of players for each number pair.

There are 66 players participating.

For **1–4**, use the rule to complete each table. Describe a feature of each pattern.

1. Rule: Multiply by 12

Number of Dozens	4	5	6	7
Number of Eggs	48		72	

2. Rule: Divide by 9

Number of Baseball Players	54	63	72	81
Number of Teams	6	7		

3. Rule: Divide by 6

Number of Legs	162	168	174	180
Number of Insects		28	29	

4. Rule: Multiply by 10

Number of Phone Numbers	33	34	35	36
Number of Digits in Phone Numbers	330	340		

5. The table shows the amounts of money Emma earns for different numbers of chores. How much money does Emma earn when she does 6 chores?

Rule: Multiply by 9

Number of Chores	Amount Earned
3	$27
4	$36
5	$45
6	

6. enVision® STEM A *wavelength* is the distance between 1 peak of a wave of light, heat, or other energy to the next peak. Greta measured the distance for 3 wavelengths. What is distance for 1 wavelength?

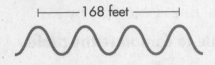

7. Write 894,217 in expanded form and using number names.

8. There are 21,611 more students enrolled in elementary school than in middle school in a city district. If there are 16,247 students enrolled in middle school, how many are enrolled in elementary school?

For **9–10**, the rule is "Divide by 7."

9. Using the rule from the table, how many T-shirts would sell for $168?

Do you need to find the price of 30 T-shirts and 9 T-shirts to solve Exercise 10?

10. Higher Order Thinking How much more do 30 T-shirts cost than 9 T-shirts? Explain.

	Price	Number of T-Shirts
DATA	$147	21
	$154	22
	$161	23

✓ **Assessment Practice**

11. There are 24 hours in a day. Use the rule "Multiply by 24" to show the relationship between the number of days and the number of hours. Use each digit from the box once to complete the table.

Number of Days	13	14	15	16	17
Number of Hours	□□□	336	360	384	□□□

0	1
2	3
4	8

Name _____

Another Look!

Alan is using the rule below to make a repeating pattern. What is the 31st shape in Alan's pattern?

Rule: Rectangle, Circle, Square, Triangle

...

Divide: $31 \div 4 = 7 R3$

The pattern repeats 7 times. Then 3 more shapes appear.

The third shape in the repeating pattern is the square.
The square is the 31st shape in the repeating pattern.

Every fourth shape is the same because there are four repeating items in the pattern.

For **1–4**, draw or write the next three items to continue each repeating pattern.

1. The rule is "Oval, Triangle."

...

2. The rule is "Short, Tall, Medium."

...

3. The rule is "2, 8, 9."

2, 8, 9, 2, 8, 9, 2, 8, 9, …

4. The rule is "1, 2, 3, 4, 5."

1, 2, 3, 4, 5, 1, 2, 3, 4, …

For **5–8**, determine the given shape or number in each repeating pattern.

5. The rule is "Star, Circle, Heart." What is the 17th shape?

...

6. The rule is "Add, Subtract, Multiply, Divide." What is the 100th shape?

...

7. The rule is "1, 1, 1, 2." What is the 87th number?

1, 1, 1, 2, 1, 1, 1, 2, 1, 1, 1, 2, …

8. The rule is "8, 9." What is the 100th number?

8, 9, 8, 9, 8, 9, …

9. Stonehenge is an ancient monument in England thought to have been originally made up of a repeating pattern of rocks that looks like this:

The rule is "Vertical, Horizontal, Vertical." Draw the 26th shape in the pattern.

10. Reasoning Marcia is using the rule "Heart, Star, Star" to make a repeating pattern. She wants the pattern to repeat 6 times. How many stars will be in Marcia's pattern?

11. A-Z Vocabulary Describe the difference between *perimeter* and *area*.

12. Higher Order Thinking Tanji creates a "Square, Circle" repeating pattern. Kenji creates a "Square, Circle, Triangle, Circle" repeating pattern. If both Tanji and Kenji have 100 shapes in their patterns, which pattern contains more circles? Explain.

Tanji's Pattern

Kenji's Pattern

✓ **Assessment Practice**

13. Which rules give a repeating pattern that has a 9 as the 20th number? Select all that apply.

☐ 1, 9, 4
☐ 1, 2, 3, 9
☐ 9, 9, 9
☐ 1, 2, 9
☐ 9, 1, 4

14. Which rules give a repeating pattern that has a circle as the 20th shape? Select all that apply.

☐ Square, Circle
☐ Circle, Square, Triangle
☐ Trapezoid, Circle, Square
☐ Circle, Circle, Circle
☐ Circle, Triangle, Circle

Name _____

Another Look!

Dwayne built the towers shown. He used the rule that each tower has 1 more block than the tower before it. How many blocks are needed for the 10th tower?

Tell how you can solve the problem.

- I can use the rule that describes how objects or values in a pattern are related.

- I can use features of the pattern not stated in the rule to extend the pattern.

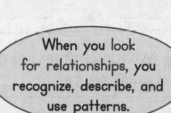

Tower 1   Tower 2   Tower 3   Tower 4

Extend the pattern and find features not stated in the rule.

When you look for relationships, you recognize, describe, and use patterns.

Tower Number	1	2	3	4	5
Number of Blocks	2	3	4	5	6

The number of blocks in a tower is 1 more than the tower number. The 10th tower contains $10 + 1 = 11$ blocks.

Use Structure

Sarah is making diamond shapes with yarn like the ones shown. She adds the lengths of the sides to determine how much yarn she needs. What is the greatest side length Sarah could make with 48 inches of yarn? Use Exercises 1–3 to answer the question.

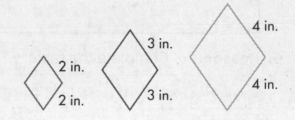

1. Complete the table to help describe the pattern.

Inches on One Side	2	3	4	5	6
Inches of Yarn Needed	8	12	16		

2. What is another feature of the pattern that is not described in the rule?

3. What is the side length of the diamond Sarah can make with 48 inches of yarn? Explain.

Swimming Pools

Pete's Pools installs rectangular pools that are all 10 feet wide. The length can vary from 10 feet to 30 feet. The company installed a pool with a perimeter of 76 feet. What was the length of the pool?

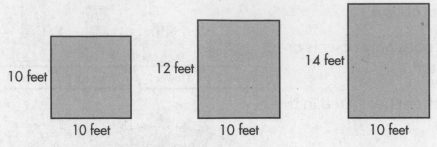

10 feet · 10 feet · 12 feet · 10 feet · 14 feet · 10 feet

4. **Reasoning** What quantities are given in the problem and what do the numbers mean?

5. **Make Sense and Persevere** What do you need to find?

6. **Reasoning** Complete the table.

Length in Feet	10	12	14	16	18	20	22	24
Perimeter	40	44	48					

7. **Use Structure** What is the length of a pool with a perimeter of 76 feet? Explain how you found the answer. Then describe how you can use a feature of the pattern to find the length.

> When you use structure, you break the problem into simpler parts.

Name _____

Additional Practice 15-2
Understand Angles and Unit Angles

Another Look!

You can find the measure of an angle using fractions of a circle.

The angle shown is $\frac{2}{5}$ of a circle.

What is the measure of this angle?

Remember that $\frac{2}{5} = \frac{1}{5} + \frac{1}{5}$.
Divide to find the angle measure of $\frac{1}{5}$ of a circle.

$360° \div 5 = 72°$

An angle that turns through $\frac{1}{5}$ of a circle measures 72°.

$72° + 72° = 144°$

The measure of this angle is 144°.

Fractions of a circle can help with the understanding of angle measures.

For **1–4**, find the measure of each angle.

1. The angle turns through $\frac{1}{9}$ of the circle.

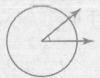

2. A circle is divided into 6 equal parts. What is the total angle measure of 1 part?

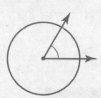

_____ ÷ 6 = _____

3. A circle is divided into 5 equal parts. What is the total angle measure of 4 parts?

4. A circle is divided into 8 equal parts. What is the total angle measure of 4 parts?

5. Noah used a bar diagram to find the measure of an angle that turns through $\frac{1}{5}$ of a circle. Write an equation to find the measure of the angle.

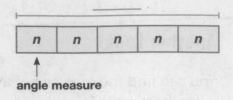

| n | n | n | n | n |

↑
angle measure

---

6. Number Sense Miguel cut $\frac{1}{4}$ from a round pie. Mariah cut a piece from the same pie with an angle measure of 60°. Who cut the larger piece? Explain.

7. Construct Arguments Janie served 4 same-size pizzas at the class party. Explain how to find how many slices of pizza Janie served if the angle for each slice turns through a right angle.

---

8. Wendy's older brother is buying a car. He can make 24 payments of $95 or 30 payments of $80 each. Which costs less? How much less?

9. Higher Order Thinking A circle is divided into 18 equal parts. How many degrees is the angle measure for each part? How many degrees is the angle measure for 5 of those parts? Break apart 18 to solve. Explain.

✓ **Assessment Practice**

10. Which angle measure is represented by the shaded part of the circle?

Ⓐ 90°
Ⓑ 120°
Ⓒ 144°
Ⓓ 60°

11. Which angle measure is represented by the clock hands?

Ⓐ 90°
Ⓑ 120°
Ⓒ 144°
Ⓓ 60°

Practice Video Tools Games

Another Look!

The smaller angle of the tan pattern block measures 30°.

Use the tan pattern block to find the measure of the angle below.

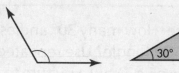

You can use an angle you know to find the measure of an angle you do not know.

Four of the 30° angles will fit into the angle.

$30° + 30° + 30° + 30° = 120°$
The measure of this angle is 120°.
It turns through 120 one-degree angles.

For **1–6**, find the measure of each angle. Use pattern blocks to help.

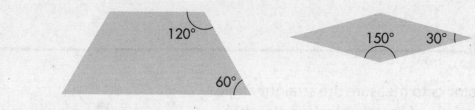

1.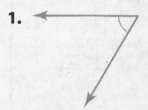

2.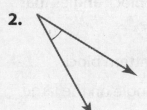

3.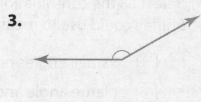

4.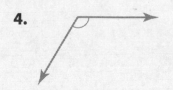

5.

6.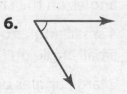

7. **Construct Arguments** A round classroom table is made from 5 identical wedges. What is the measure of each angle formed at the center of the classroom table? Explain.

8. How many unit angles does the smaller angle of a small pattern block turn through? Explain.

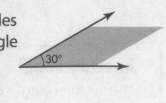

9. Mario cut a circular pizza into 9 equal slices. He put a slice of pizza on each of 5 plates. What is the measure for the angle of the slices that are left?

10. **Number Sense** How many 30° angles are there in a 150° angle? Use repeated subtraction to solve. Draw a picture to justify your solution.

11. Matt's parents pay him $5.50 for each half hour he babysits his sister, plus a two dollar tip. If Matt made $18.50, for how long did he babysit?

12. **Higher Order Thinking** If a clock face reads 1:00, how many hours must pass for the hands to form a straight angle?

✓ **Assessment Practice**

13. Shirley uses pattern blocks to measure the straight angle. Select all the combinations of pattern block angles that Shirley could use to measure the angle.

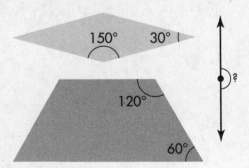

- ☐ 6 small angles on the small pattern block
- ☐ 1 large angle and one small angle on the large pattern block
- ☐ 1 large angle on the large pattern block and 3 small angles on the small pattern block
- ☐ 4 small angles on the small pattern block and one small angle on the large pattern block
- ☐ 2 large angles on the large pattern block

Practice Video Tools Games

Another Look!

To measure an angle:

Place the protractor's center on the vertex of the angle and the 0° mark on one of the angle's rays. Read the number in degrees where the other ray of the angle crosses the protractor. If the angle is acute, use the lesser number. If the angle is obtuse, use the greater number.

To draw an angle:

Draw a dot to show the vertex of the angle. Place the center of the protractor on the vertex point. Draw another point at the 0° mark and another point at the angle degree mark. Draw rays from the vertex through the other points.

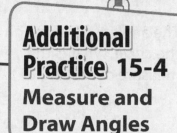

You can use a protractor to measure or draw angles.

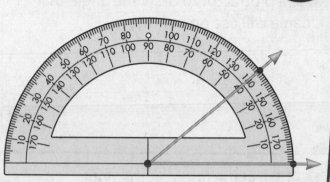

For **1–4**, measure each angle. Tell if each angle is acute, right, or obtuse.

1.

2.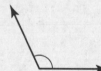

3.

4.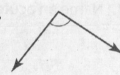

For **5–12**, use a protractor to draw an angle for each measure.

5. 75°

6. 80°

7. 155°

8. 45°

9. 135°

10. 180°

11. 5°

12. 90°

13. The angle turns through $\frac{1}{5}$ of the circle. What is the measure of the angle?

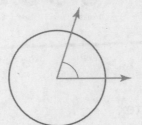

There are multiple ways to determine an angle's measure.

---

14. Joanie is making a map of the trails in the community park. Two of the trails start at the same point and form a 40° angle. Use a protractor to draw the angle that Joanie will use on her map.

15. **enVision®** STEM Watts, volts, and amps are used to measure electricity. There is a formula that shows the relationship between watts, volts, and amps. Volts × Amps = Watts. If the volts are 120 and the amps are 5, how many watts are there?

For **16–18**, use the figure at the right.

16. Does the measure of ∠COA equal the measure of ∠EOD? What are their measures?

17. Name an acute, an obtuse, and a right angle.

18. **Higher Order Thinking** The measure of ∠EOF is 35°. The measure of ∠FOB is 120°. What is the measure of ∠BOC?

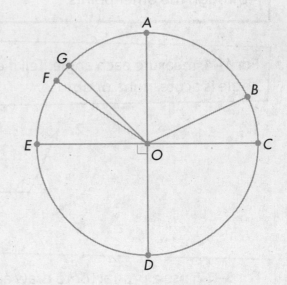

✓ **Assessment Practice**

19. Which angle measures 25°?

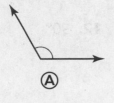

Ⓐ

Ⓑ

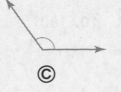

Ⓒ

Ⓓ

Practice Video Tools Games

Another Look!

When light hits a mirror, it reflects at the same angle as it hits. In the diagram shown, ∠ABC has the same measure as ∠CBD, where $\overline{BC}$ makes a right angle with the mirror.

Measure ∠ABC. Then, write and solve an equation to find the measure of ∠DBE.

Tell how you can strategically choose a tool to solve the problem.

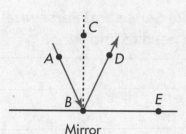

Mirror

• I can decide which tool is appropriate.

• I can explain why it is the best tool to use.

• I can use the tool correctly.

The measure of ∠ABC is 25°. The measure of ∠CBD is also 25° and the sum of ∠CBD and ∠DBE is 90°.
So, $25° + d = 90°$, $d = 90° - 25° = 65°$.
The measure of ∠DBE is 65°.

Use Appropriate Tools

Jason wants to set up blocks for a game. He wants to set up the blocks in an array, so there are the same number of rows as columns. He wants to use between 20 and 90 blocks. How can Jason set up the blocks? Use Exercises 1–2 to help solve.

1. What tool could Jason use? Explain how Jason could use the tool to find at least one way to set up the blocks.

When you use appropriate tools, you consider options before selecting a tool.

Available Tools
Place-value blocks
Fraction strips
Rulers
Grid paper
Counters

2. What are all the ways Jason can set up the blocks?

Tiling

Marcus created the tile pattern shown. All the angles of each hexagon have the same measure and all the angles of each equilateral triangle have the same measure. Find the measure of each angle.

3. **Make Sense and Persevere** What do you know and what do you need to find?

4. **Use Appropriate Tools** What tool could you use to measure the angle of a hexagon? Explain how to use the tool you chose. What is the measure?

When you use appropriate tools, you use the tool you chose correctly.

5. **Model with Math** Write and solve an equation which could be used to find the measure of one angle of a triangle. What is the measure of the angle? Explain.

Name _____

Another Look!

You can use geometric terms to describe what you draw.

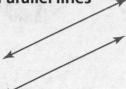

Parallel lines

Intersecting lines

Perpendicular lines

Parallel lines never intersect.

Intersecting lines pass through the same point.

Perpendicular lines form right angles.

For **1–3**, use geometric terms to describe what is shown. Be as specific as possible.

1.
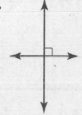

2.
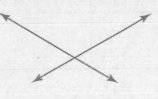

3.
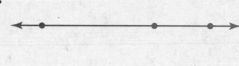

For **4–7**, use the figure at the right.

4. Name three different lines.

5. Name a pair of parallel lines.

6. Name two lines that are perpendicular.

7. Name two intersecting lines that are not perpendicular.

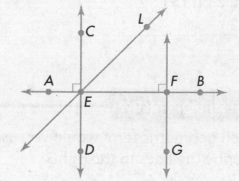

8. Name two lines.

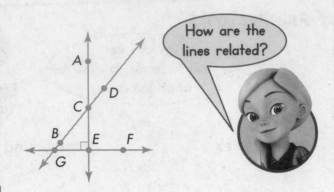

How are the lines related?

9. Name two lines that are perpendicular.

10. Draw a line $\overleftrightarrow{HF}$ on the diagram that is parallel to $\overleftrightarrow{AE}$ and perpendicular to $\overleftrightarrow{GF}$.

---

11. **A-Z Vocabulary** Draw and describe a point. What real-world object could you use as a model of a point?

12. **Critique Reasoning** Ali says if two lines share a point, they cannot be parallel. Do you agree? Explain.

---

13. Draw and label parallel lines $\overleftrightarrow{XY}$ and $\overleftrightarrow{RS}$. Then draw and label $\overleftrightarrow{TS}$ so it is perpendicular to both $\overleftrightarrow{XY}$ and $\overleftrightarrow{RS}$. Draw point Z on $\overleftrightarrow{TS}$.

14. **Higher Order Thinking** $\overleftrightarrow{RS}$ is perpendicular to $\overleftrightarrow{TU}$. $\overleftrightarrow{RS}$ is parallel to $\overleftrightarrow{VW}$. What is the relationship between $\overleftrightarrow{TU}$ and $\overleftrightarrow{VW}$? Draw lines if needed.

✓ Assessment Practice

15. Which geometric term would you use to describe the lines to the right?

Think about the relationship between the two lines.

    Ⓐ   Perpendicular lines

    Ⓑ   Point A

    Ⓒ   Parallel lines

    Ⓓ   Intersecting lines

Name _____

Additional Practice 16-2
Classify Triangles

Another Look!

Triangles can be classified by their angle measures, side lengths, or both.

Equilateral triangle
All sides are the same length.

Isosceles triangle
At least two sides are the same length.

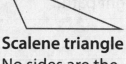

Scalene triangle
No sides are the same length.

Right triangle
One angle is a right angle.

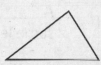

Acute triangle
All three angles are acute angles.

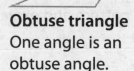

Obtuse triangle
One angle is an obtuse angle.

For **1–6**, classify each triangle by its sides and then by its angles.

1.
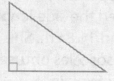

2.

3.
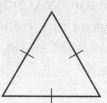

4.
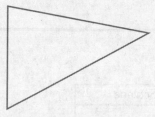

5.
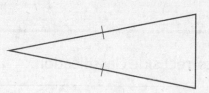

6.
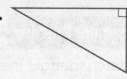

For **7–8**, use the figure at the right.

7. Hilary flew from Denver to Atlanta for business. From Atlanta, she flew to Chicago to visit her aunt. From Chicago, she flew back home to Denver. Classify the triangle made by her complete flight path.

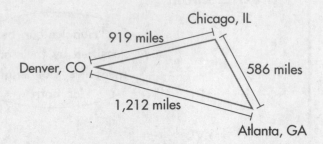

8. What is the perimeter of the triangle made by Hilary's flight path?

9. **Algebra** A pattern follows the rule: acute triangle, obtuse triangle, acute triangle, obtuse triangle…. It also follows the rule: equilateral, scalene, equilateral, scalene… Draw a triangle that could be the sixth shape in the pattern and explain.

10. **Vocabulary** Fill in the blanks to correctly complete the sentences:

A _____ triangle has no sides the same length.

A triangle with one 90° angle is called a _____ triangle.

An isosceles triangle has ____ sides the same length.

11. **Critique Reasoning** Sylvia says a right triangle can have only one right angle. Joel says a right triangle can have more than one right angle. Who is correct? Explain.

12. **Higher Order Thinking** Dani measured the angles of a triangle as 120°, 36°, and 24°. Then, she measured the side lengths as 25.3 cm, 17.2 cm, and 11.8 cm. She said her triangle is an isosceles obtuse triangle. Do you agree? Explain.

☑ Assessment Practice

13. Draw each triangle in its correct side classification.

Isosceles	Equilateral	Scalene

Name _____

Additional Practice 16-3
Classify Quadrilaterals

Another Look!

Quadrilaterals can be named for their angles and sides.

Quadrilateral
A polygon with 4 sides.

Rectangle
There are four right angles and opposite sides are parallel.

Parallelogram
Opposite sides are parallel.

Square
There are four right angles. All sides are the same length.

Rhombus
Opposite sides are parallel and all sides are the same length.

Trapezoid
There is only one pair of parallel sides.

For **1–4**, write the most specific name for each quadrilateral.

1.

2.

3.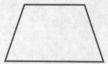

4.

For **5–7**, write all the names possible for each quadrilateral.

5.

6.

7.

8. The figure at the right is called an Escher cube. It is named after the Dutch artist M.C. Escher. Look at the 7 white shapes created by this drawing. Name each shape.

9. Mr. Meyer draws a shape on the board. It has 4 sides of equal length and 4 right angles. List all of the names possible to describe the shape Mr. Meyer drew.

10. Generalize Why can a square never be a trapezoid?

11. Rick drew a rhombus. What names might describe the figure based on what you know about quadrilaterals? Explain.

12. Higher Order Thinking Hannah has 11 toothpicks that are the same length. Name the different types of triangles and quadrilaterals Hannah can make if she uses only one toothpick for each side of each figure.

✅ **Assessment Practice**

13. Is this statement below true? Write an explanation for how you would classify the shape.

A quadrilateral has 4 right angles, so it is a square.

Think about which types of quadrilaterals have 4 right angles.

Another Look!

> Line-symmetric figures are figures that can be folded to make matching parts.

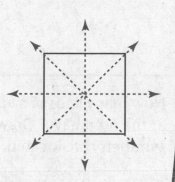

How many lines of symmetry does a square have?

If you fold the square along any of the 4 dashed lines, the two matching parts will lie on top of each other.

A square has 4 lines of symmetry. It is a line-symmetric figure.

For **1–4**, tell if each line is a line of symmetry.

1.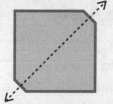

2.

3.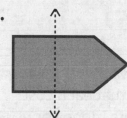

4.

For **5–12**, decide if each figure is line symmetric. Draw and tell how many lines of symmetry each figure has.

5.

6.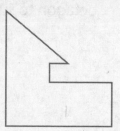

7.

8.

9.

10.

11.

12.

13. **Construct Arguments** How many lines of symmetry does a scalene triangle have? Explain.

14. **Reasoning** Can an isosceles triangle have three lines of symmetry? Explain.

15. How many lines of symmetry does the wagon wheel at the right have? Draw or explain where the lines of symmetry are located.

16. **Number Sense** Stuart has $23.75. He wants to buy 2 tickets that each cost $15.75. How much more money does Stuart need? Use bills and coins to solve.

17. **Higher Order Thinking** Regular polygons have sides that are all the same length and angles that all have the same measure. A regular pentagon has 5 lines of symmetry and a regular hexagon has 6 lines of symmetry. Make a conjecture about the number of lines of symmetry for a regular octagon. Draw a regular octagon to support your conjecture.

18. Which of the following numbers has exactly 2 lines of symmetry?

  Ⓐ 1

  Ⓑ 3

  Ⓒ 7

  Ⓓ 8

19. Which of the following letters is **NOT** line symmetric?

  Ⓐ W

  Ⓑ T

  Ⓒ S

  Ⓓ A

Practice Video Tools Games

Another Look!

You can use dot paper to draw line-symmetric figures.

How to draw a line-symmetric figure:

Step 1

Draw a figure on dot paper.

Step 2

Draw a line of symmetry.

Step 3

Complete the figure on the opposite side of the line of symmetry.

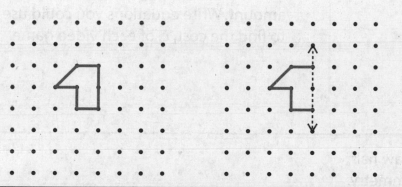

For **1–6**, use the line of symmetry to draw a line-symmetric figure.

1.

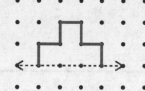

2.

3.

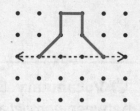

4.

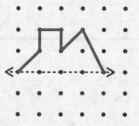

5.

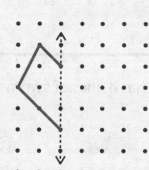

6.

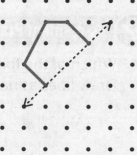

7. Draw a quadrilateral that has no lines of symmetry.

8. Draw a quadrilateral with exactly 2 lines of symmetry.

9. A storage compartment for a gym locker room can hold up to 7 folded towels. Katie has 150 towels to fold and put away. How many compartments will be filled? How many towels will be in a compartment that is not completely filled?

10. Model with Math James bought $175 in accessories for his video game console. He spent $15 on a new power cord and the rest of his money on 5 new video games. Each video game cost the same amount. Write equations you could use to find the cost, c, of each video game.

11. Create a line symmetric figure. Draw half of a figure. Then draw a line of symmetry. Complete your figure on the opposite side of the line of symmetry.

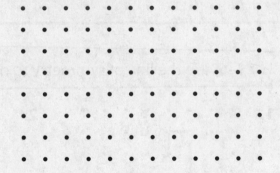

12. **Vocabulary** Describe the difference between *parallel* and *intersecting lines*.

13. Higher Order Thinking Draw a figure that is not a quadrilateral and has two lines of symmetry, one horizontal and one vertical.

14. Which of the following figures has 4 lines of symmetry? Draw lines as needed.

Ⓐ Ⓑ Ⓒ Ⓓ

Practice   Video   Tools   Games

Another Look!

Alisa said all obtuse triangles have acute angles because you cannot draw an obtuse triangle with all obtuse angles. Critique Alisa's reasoning.

Tell how you can critique the reasoning of others.

- I can look for flaws in her reasoning.

- I can decide whether all cases have been considered.

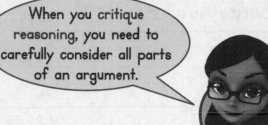

When you critique reasoning, you need to carefully consider all parts of an argument.

Decide whether or not you think Alisa's statement is true. Then, explain why.

Alisa is correct. All obtuse triangles have one obtuse angle that is greater than 90°. The remaining angles are acute. An obtuse triangle cannot have a right angle.

Critique Reasoning

Ronnie said that if all of the sides of a polygon have equal length, then all of the angles will have the same measure. He drew the figures shown.

1. Describe at least one thing you could do to critique Ronnie's reasoning.

2. Does Ronnie's reasoning make sense? Explain.

Rachel said the sum of three odd numbers is always odd. She gave the examples shown.

3. Describe at least one thing you could do to critique Rachel's reasoning

4. Does Rachel's reasoning make sense? Explain.

	Rachel
$5 + 3 + 7 = 15$	
$21 + 33 + 45 = 99$	
$127 + 901 + 65 = 1,093$	

Designing a Logo

Tamara was asked to design a logo for the Writing
Club. The logo needs to be a scalene triangle.
Tamara reasons about how to draw the logo.
Critique Tamara's reasoning.

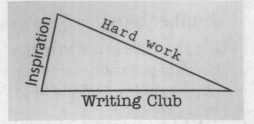

5. **Make Sense and Persevere** What do you know, and
what do you need to do?

Tamara's Reasoning
A scalene triangle has 3 sides
of differing lengths. Each of
the angles is acute because
I cannot draw a triangle with
3 different right angles or
3 different obtuse angles.

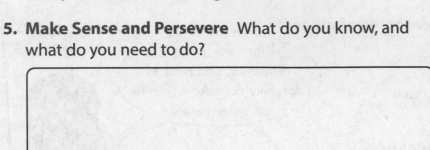

6. **Critique Reasoning** Critique Tamara's reasoning.
What can you do to improve her reasoning?

When you critique
reasoning you carefully read
someone else's argument.

7. **Use Structure** Can Tamara draw a scalene triangle with
line symmetry? Explain.

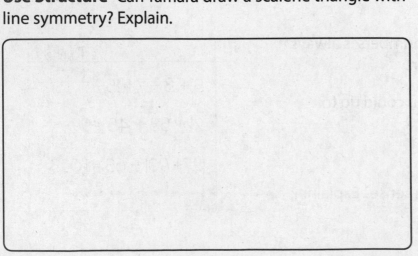

enVision® Mathematics

Photographs

Every effort has been made to secure permission and provide appropriate credit for photographic material. The publisher deeply regrets any omission and pledges to correct errors called to its attention in subsequent editions.

Unless otherwise acknowledged, all photographs are the property of Savvas Learning Company LLC.

Photo locators denoted as follows: Top (T), Center (C), Bottom (B), Left (L), Right (R), Background (Bkgd)

114 Africa Studio/Fotolia; **130** (L) Yaping/Shutterstock, (C) Melinda Fawver/Shutterstock, (R) Undy/Fotolia. **168** Viorel Sima/Shutterstock.